MW00830649

FISH FOOD

A Fly Fisher's Guide to Bugs and Bait

Ralph Cutter

Illustrated by Lisa Cutter

Photographs by Ralph Cutter

STACKPOLE
BOOKS

0 11557 03219 2

Copyright © 2005 by Stackpole Books

Published by
STACKPOLE BOOKS
5067 Ritter Road
Mechanicsburg, PA 17055
www.stackpolebooks.com

All rights reserved, including the right to reproduce this book or
portions thereof in any form or by any means, electronic or mechanical,
including photocopying, recording, or by any information storage and
retrieval system, without permission in writing from the publisher.
All inquiries should be addressed to Stackpole Books, 5067 Ritter Road,
Mechanicsburg, Pennsylvania 17055.

Printed in China

First edition

10 9 8 7 6 5 4 3 2

Cover art by Lisa Cutter
Cover design by Caroline Stover

Library of Congress Cataloging-in-Publication Data
Cutter, Ralph, 1955-
  Fish food : a fly fisher's guide to bugs and bait / Ralph Cutter ;
illustrated by Lisa Cutter ; photographs by the Ralph Cutter.
    p. cm.
  Includes index.
  ISBN 0-8117-3219-3 (alk. paper)
  1. Fishing baits. 2. Trout—Food. I. Title.

SH448.C88 2005
799.17'57—dc22
                                                              2004027290
ISBN 978-0-8117-3219-2

Dedicated to
Roland Knapp

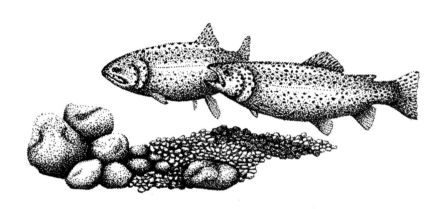

Contents

Foreword

Those of us of a certain age remember a time when "matching the hatch"—if we deigned to match it at all—consisted merely of inspecting an insect perched on the water's surface and then choosing some generic pattern such as an Adams or a Quill Gordon to imitate it. Which we didn't—imitate, that is. At best, we were within the proverbial ballpark with regard to size and, perhaps, color. That we still caught trout when the fish were actually keying on emergers or spinners said more for our quarry's occasional profound stupidity than it did for the supposed insight of the angler.

Over the years, however, the base of knowledge on which our sport is built has grown tremendously. Walk into a fly shop now, and you're confronted with bins holding parachute-style mayflies, no-hackles, cripples, beadhead nymphs, vernille worms (worms!), and giant foam-bodied ants. All of which speaks to one of the underlying truths of fly fishing: To fish well, you have to be willing to observe and adapt. The plethora of fly patterns now available, the concurrent evolutions in tackle and tactics, are the direct result of observation and adaptation.

Those of us who fish California's waters have long recognized that one of the masters of observation and adaptation is Ralph Cutter. His *Sierra Trout Guide*, first published more than two decades ago, remains the essential text not just for anglers who seek success in John Muir's Range of Light, but for anyone who wants to learn the natural histories of its fish. His popular column on trout foods in *California Fly Fisher* magazine has helped innumerable anglers fish smarter. Ralph is known for snorkeling rivers and lakes and for traveling vast distances by foot and by vehicle, the better to understand the habits of aquatic predator and prey. This curiosity, along with a willingness to experiment, has led to innovations in fly design and angling techniques. (Ralph's E/C Caddis is now my go-to pattern for most waters.)

Ralph Cutter is a fly fisher's fly fisher: an expert at handling a fly rod, certainly, but also inquisitive and, just as important, iconoclastic. As you'll learn from this book, he takes nothing for granted. And the knowledge you'll gain from Ralph's hard work will surely improve your ability to tempt trout to your fly.

Richard Anderson
California Fly Fisher
Truckee, California
September 16, 2004

Preface

The goal of this book is to stop you from fishing . . . stop you from fishing long enough to open your eyes and question reality. It wasn't so long ago that common knowledge supported the belief that flies evolved from rotting meat. I fished for decades content in the notion that, like flies spontaneously emerging from a bloated cat, little yellow stoneflies emerged from midstream. How could they *not*? All my fishing friends said they did, and I spent countless summer evenings watching the little bugs pop out of the water and flutter away to the freedom of the skies.

In the midst of one such hatch, I stopped fishing long enough to stretch a seine across the film to sample the insect population. A short while later, I pulled the soggy net to shore and counted the bugs. There were some leaves, a clot of algae, and a stick. There were also half a dozen mayfly nymph exoskeletons, some caddisflies, and a bunch of bedraggled little yellow stoneflies. It wasn't until several days later that it dawned on me there were no stonefly nymph shucks in the net—there should have been dozens.

Careful observations both above and below the water surface revealed that the little yellow stoneflies were not emergers at all, but egg layers that had landed on the water and were floating downstream, wings flush with the film and virtually invisible from an angler's perspective. At a moment of spontaneous motivation, the little yellow stones would leap into view and fly away like the perfect emergers they weren't. The knowledge changed my fishing approach, led to more trout hooked, and best of all, made me pause to smile at our little secret every time I watched the bugs bust off a river.

I hope the stuff in this book will make you smile; bugs aren't boring, so learning about them shouldn't be. Most people will thumb the pages in hopes of becoming a more "successful" angler. If that describes you—perfect! I'm confident the words will shepherd you to bigger fish and more of them; my *hope*, however, is that the words will reshape your meaning of a successful day on the water. Bugs are pretty damn cool, and sometimes watching a hatch is more fulfilling than fishing it.

Some of what you read will be contrary to approved notions; maybe it's because I'm a contrary guy, or perhaps because my perception of reality is damaged from too many decades spent breathing underwater. Maybe it's because approved notions are just that: notions rather than critically observed phenomena.

Some of what you read will be repetitive. This is a compilation of columns written for *California Fly Fisher* magazine, and all too frequently I reaffirm or rediscover my own discoveries. I'm afraid to count the number of times the reader is urged to coat his wet fly with dry-fly floatant. I could dream of something else to say, but in my experience, the value of a shimmering nymph bears repeating over and over again.

Some of what you read in this book will be wrong or at least open to interpretation. Error is almost always the result of attempting to fold the behavior of fish and their foods into neat factoids without providing wriggle room for regional variances or individual behavior. Peruse the chapter on *Callibaetis*, and then flip to the end of the book and read "Beneath the Mirror." You'll see what I mean. Learn from my mistakes as well as my observations. Take it from there, observe and take notes, then write your own book. I can't wait to read it!

Ralph Cutter
Nevada City, California
October 2004

Acknowledgments

Gary LaFontaine was the catalyst that made me look at the underwater world with a critical eye. Upon release of *Caddisflies* in 1981, some well-known fly-fishing "experts" heaped scorn on his observations. It was Gary who persuaded me to dive with a camera and eventually video gear to document the experience for those unwilling to believe what happens "beneath the mirror."

Cheerleader to the end, Gary goaded me into starting this book, and his midnight phone calls of encouragement and scolding were hard to ignore. After his untimely death, I put the manuscript on a shelf. A year later, Judith Schnell revitalized the idea by suggesting we use the *California Fly Fisher* columns as a platform. Gary would have been thrilled. Thanks to both of you.

Today is October 1, 2004, the deadline for the next aquatic ecology column in *California Fly Fisher* magazine. I don't have a clue what it is going to be about, much less have it written. I am expecting an e-mail at any moment from Richard Anderson asking where the piece is. It is a ritual we go through with every publication. Through Richard's tireless prodding, the slacker in me is forced to overcome inertia and write a column every six weeks. This book is a compilation of many of those columns, and without Richard's cajoling, threats, and ultimate patience, there isn't a chance in the world this thing ever would have been written.

Phil Takatsuno is the Japanese brother I never had. At a moment's notice (sometimes without any notice at all), Lisa and I will knock on the door of his West Yellowstone home and have a base of operations from which to dive, film, and watch bugs.

Sometimes we even fish. We've spent literal months mooching off of Phil, and never once has he suggested we leave. Thanks, bud.

Rusty Vorous has been our partner in crime more times than I can count (some I can't remember at all). No one has more enthusiasm for the subaquatic world than Rusty. As a dirt-broke fishing guide some twenty years ago, Rusty coughed up an unbelievable sum for an underwater Nikonos camera to shoot aquatic insects. It didn't faze him in the least that he didn't know how to swim. Today still, his curiosity and infectious enthusiasm are unabated. When I need a dose of "rattle squirt," it's Rusty I turn to. I owe him more than a lifetime supply of Tanqueray.

Dr. Roland Knapp, to whom this book is dedicated, has committed his life to making this planet a better place. Roland is one of the few scientists today who can honestly live under the banner of naturalist. A fish biologist by training (his interest in fish sparked by chasing golden trout with a fly rod), Roland is a cutting-edge herpetologist whose Sierra Nevada studies have carried him deep into the realms of ornithology, entomology, and just about every other ology worth knowing about. Roland is more than just a close friend and mentor. He is who I want to be when I grow up.

Every sentence in this book reflects some part of Lisa's support and effort. To be honest, there were many times that donning a cold, slimy wetsuit and slipping into the water was pretty close to the bottom of the list of things I wanted to do. Without Lisa, those times were a chore; with her, they became outings or picnics. On top of being my one-person support team, fielding phone calls, changing scuba bottles, or surprising me with a bottle of wine when I came up for air, she dedicated countless hours to drawing the sketchings that appear in the book. No words can express my love and gratitude for Lisa's companionship. The best I can do is simply say, "I love you," because I do.

PART ONE

Know Your Ingredients

1

In the Beginning

This is the first chapter, so let's start at the beginning. Let's start at a place in time before there were fish, much less fishermen. In this time, there weren't even dinosaurs. It was the Age of Insects.

In this age, hawk-size dragonflies chased mayflies sporting wings taller than puppies. Cave children cowered in their shadows. This was a long time ago . . . two to three hundred million years ago, to be exact.

The life process for these bugs was simple. They ate, mated, and laid eggs. The eggs hatched into nymphs that, if you squinted your eyes real hard, would have looked pretty similar to the adults. These nymphs had six legs, three body parts (head, thorax, and abdomen), and buds on their backs containing nascent wings. They didn't have internal skeletons, but their chitinous skin gave them structural integrity and prevented their guts from spilling out all over the place.

This skin, or exoskeleton, was good, but it had a major fault: It didn't grow. As the insect grew, the exoskeleton would stretch

An insect has a hard exoskeleton that must be molted periodically as the bug inside grows. The exoskeleton has split on the thorax of this flavilinea *mayfly nymph, and the pale "fresh" nymph is bulging out.*

The mayfly nymph has completed its molt and stands beside its discarded exoskeleton. The nymph will spend the next several hours darkening and hardening.

and distort and finally split open between the shoulders, allowing the bug within to crawl out. This process, called molt or ecdysis, would prove to be of extreme importance to fly fishers.

The freshly emerged bug was contained within a new exoskeleton that was slightly larger than the old. With each ecdysis, the newly emerged bug had larger and darker wing pads. After a dozen or so such molts, the adult, sexually mature version of the nymph would emerge wearing a set of wings in place of the wing pads. This evolution from egg to nymph to adult is called simple or incomplete metamorphosis.

Millions of insect species roamed the countryside and competed vigorously among themselves for food, real estate, and luscious mates. Choice niches were occupied by those insects best adapted to each niche. Ripe fruits high in a tree were garnered by those bugs adapted to flying high. Nutritious algae beds in fast, turbulent waters were harvested by those insects with strong, clingy legs and low, sleek profiles. Insects specializing in chasing down and devouring other bugs became strong of jaw and fast of wing. Over the eons, a wonderful order evolved.

Somewhere in the scheme of things, a group of insects radically changed its means of development. Instead of evolving from egg to nymph and then on into the adult forms, their eggs hatched into soft-bodied, wormlike creatures, known as larvae. Freed from their lifelong nymphal templates, these larvae could utilize previously bypassed niches.

The larvae exploited every conceivable space. They roamed the crystalline brooks, springs, and tarns of the world's tallest mountains. They burrowed into muck, feces, and putrefied flesh. They basked in sulfurous hot springs and bathed under arctic snowfields.

Regardless of which habitat the larvae chose to occupy, all entered a period of pupation from which would evolve the adult form. Some pupae, such as the cocoons of moths, remained tightly fixed to a single location; others, like the caddisfly pupae, could move about quickly and efficiently.

Unlike the adults of incomplete metamorphosis, which looked closely akin to their nymphal selves, the adults of complete metamorphosis were limited only by the whim of evolution. Creatures as diverse as swallowtail butterflies and carrion beetles shared the common bond of complete metamorphosis.

All of today's insects undergo either complete or incomplete metamorphosis (see table). During a hatch, the differences between the two in both appearance and behavior are profound. Many anglers are educated to the point of discriminating among nymph, larva, and pupal fly patterns. The fly shops have taught us well, because they have a vested interest in filling our boxes with a complete assortment of these flies.

How many anglers actually understand the vagaries of fishing these patterns? Why do we insist on calling it "nymphing" when we fish with a larval or pupal imitation? Future chapters will explore these differences and tell you exactly which flies presented in exactly which manner will best exploit these differences. In short, you will become a better angler.

INSECT METAMORPHOSIS

Incomplete	Complete
Mayflies	Caddisflies
Stoneflies	Midges, craneflies, flies
Dragonflies	Ants
Damselflies	Moths
Grasshoppers	Beetles

2

The Basic Bugs, Part I
The Subadults

The instructions that come with a stomach pump read something like this:

1. Catch a fish.
2. Pump its stomach.
3. Match your fly to the stomach contents.
4. Go fishing.

Like walking a skyline to expose snipers, it kind of makes sense until you think about it. It is smarter to figure out what the fish are eating before you start fishing. In entomological terms, you're going to *sample* the river.

Leave the stomach pump at home (or better yet, on the shelf in the fly shop), put the rod back in the truck for the time being, and take a wire mesh kitchen strainer and a plastic container with a tight-fitting lid down to the riverside. An aquarium net is often recommended, but it is only useful for skimming flotsam from the film . . . a minute segment of trout food habitat. You want something sturdy that will stand up to extreme collecting. A serious strainer is a sign of serious intent. A few scoops with a good strainer will give a quick approximation not only of what bugs are present, but more important, in what ratios.

A basic tenet of fish behavior is that fish tend to eat what there is most of. It's wonderful when browns are detonating beneath giant fluttering stoneflies, but more often than not they're rising amid the big stuff and sipping spinners. It's not that fish prefer the taste of mayflies; it's simply because spinners normally outnumber the stoneflies a hundred to one.

Pull the stickers off your new strainer, stomp on it to make it look used, and wade bravely into the nearest riffle. Next, brace the strainer against the riverbed and tip over a few rocks immediately upcurrent from it. The dislodged and disoriented critters that were hiding under said rocks will sweep helplessly into your trap. (I am not a fan of kick screens because far too much of the streambed gets unnecessarily trashed in the process of sampling.)

Inspect the strainer and you'll likely see a few creatures, but mostly it will be filled with gravel, sticks, and waterlogged leaves. Scoop a couple inches of water into the plastic container and add the booty from the strainer. If you collected from anything like a normal trout stream, you *will* be blown away by the number and diversity of creatures moving about. Freed from the pull of gravity and the slime of detritus, the sticks and gravel will have transformed into life.

Find the bugs with three distinct body parts: a head, thorax, and abdomen. The *head* will have obvious eyes and mouthparts and often antennae. The *thorax* is the segment where the legs stick out, and the *abdomen* is, well, the ass end of the bug and will usually have two or three tails sticking out of it. You have just identified the *nymphs*, the immature stage of some very important aquatic insects.

Now, find the nymphs with small structures attached along the sides of the abdomen. These might be small rods, cups, or disks, or they might look like feathers. These appendages are gills. If you didn't smash the nymphs with your macho strainer,

mayfly nymph

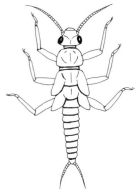

stonefly nymph

most of them will be pumping their gills to better extract oxygen from the water. You have now identified the mayfly nymphs. I don't care if they're big or small, thin or squat, or if they swim or don't swim—they're *all* immature mayflies. All mayfly nymphs have gills on their abdomens. Pretty easy, huh?

If you got the bugs from a river, in all likelihood the remainder of the nymphs are stoneflies. Stonefly nymphs may have rodlike or feathery gills between their legs or even on their necks, but never on the abdomen. (*Never* is a dangerous word. There *is* one stonefly, the *Oroperla barbara*, that does have gills on its abdomen, but unless you're exceedingly lucky, you'll

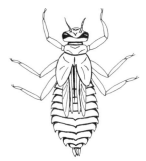

dragonfly nymph

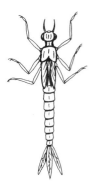

damselfly nymph

never encounter one of these rare and beautiful insects.)

If you got the nymphs from a pond or spring creek, it gets a bit trickier. Pick the nymph up and give it a gentle squeeze. If it bites and draws blood, it's probably a dragonfly nymph. These guys are *mean*.

Maybe a better idea would be to look at its tail first. If it doesn't have an obvious tail, it's likely a dragonfly nymph, water bug, or water beetle. The dragonfly nymph has a hinged, clubby-looking device under its face; this is called a *labium* and contains those nasty mouthparts. A water bug carries its forearms cocked in front of its face as if it's looking for a fight, and a beetle looks like a beetle;

With one exception, stonefly nymphs lack gills on their abdomens, whereas all mayfly nymphs do have gills.

The damselfly nymph, nearly invisible in the weeds, can de differentiated from other nymphs by its three paddle-shaped "tails." These structures (lamellae) not only scull the nymph forward, but also act as its gills.

*The **only** stonefly nymph that sports gills on the abdomen is the very rare and beautiful* Oroperla barbara.

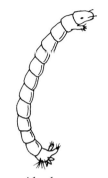

midge larva

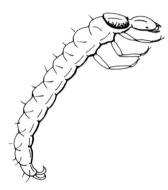

caddis larva

cased caddis

no problem there. All these guys bite, so be careful.

Another common and very beautiful nymph is the damselfly. These are easily and immediately identified by their three leaflike tails called *lamellae*. These lamellae not only aid in propulsion, but also are part of the damselfly nymph's respiratory system.

Back to the plastic container. See any pink, slender, slimy creatures that look just like worms? These are called worms. Dozens of worms are often caught in the strainer. The density of worms in a streambed can easily exceed that of any garden. The San Juan Worm isn't such a ridiculous fly after all.

The other common worm-shaped item in the strainer is likely to be Diptera larvae. Diptera is a vast group of flies that covers everything from minute midges to giant craneflies. Don't even begin to try to figure out the various Diptera larvae; even the pros get stumped. Just recognize their size, color, and relative abundance. They may come in handy someday.

By now, some of the sticks and gravel clumps in the container probably have sprouted heads and legs and are dragging themselves about. These are the caddisfly larvae. Gently remove one of the larvae from its house and examine it. It probably curled up in its nakedness, but the small *anal hooks* should be readily apparent. All caddisflies have these claws at the tip of the abdomen to help them hang on to their house or the streambed. This frees up those three pairs of legs you'll note just behind the head so that they can propel the caddis and manipulate food. The head itself is *sclerotized*, or decorated with a dark, shiny shield. Like the anal hooks, all caddis larvae have one or more *sclerotic plates*, and in the future, these will help you identify the various caddis species.

Very likely there will be caddis larvae roaming about without homes in the container. They may simply have become homeless, but more than likely these are species of free-roaming caddis that never build a case. Again, note the anal hooks, the legs, and the sclerotic plates on or behind their heads.

Did you find anything looking like yellow or green vitamin E gelcaps? These are caddisfly *puparia*. Look closely, and through the translucent skin, you'll see the developing pupae within.

Stream collectors will frequently encounter what look like vitamin E gelcaps in their screens. These are the puparia of caddisflies as they transform from larvae into the pupal stage.

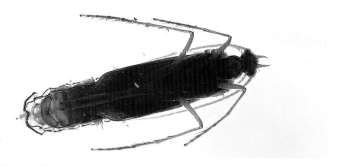

A caddisfly pupa has long swimming legs and will flop about in your strainer like a fish.

From this brief sweep of the river, you have now identified the subadult forms of all the major commonly important aquatic insect families: mayflies, stoneflies, Diptera, caddisflies, dragonflies, and damselflies. As a bonus, you're going to learn one more: the hellgrammite.

At one time or another, every bug described above has been identified to me as a hellgrammite. I don't know what made them so famous, but for being such famous bugs, no one seems to know what they look like.

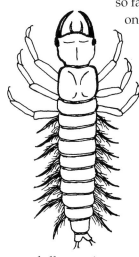

Hellgrammites are the larval stage of alderflies and dobsonflies. They are the Doberman pinschers of the water world; their bite makes a dragonfly nymph's seem like a pat on the butt. Hellgrammites live in leaf packets and under stones, usually in midelevation streams. They are long, fleshy creatures with legs and soft, pointed tubercles running along each flank. Their heads are flat and sclerotized, and they sport massive jaws that they gnash in a most menacing way. If the Japanese knew hellgrammites, Godzilla would have had six legs.

hellgrammite

Of course, there will be a few other assorted odds and ends in the strainer. You will stumble across water pennies, various pupa, beetle larvae, and even terrestrial insects that fell in the water. Set them aside for later; you already learned a bunch today.

3

The Basic Bugs, Part II
The Adults

Hunting adult bugs can be as simple as prying them off the radiator grill or as complex as setting out traps baited with ultraviolet lights and pheromones. For the budding fly-fisher entomologist, probably the best method is hanging out by the riverside with a butterfly net, a collecting jar, and a six-pack.

Butterfly nets can be found at drug and variety stores for around ten bucks. They'll work just fine, but if you want to delve seriously into the wacky world of bug collecting, I'd suggest getting an industrial-grade model. The cool bug nets have light-weight handles (some extendable), sturdy rims, and strong, reinforced nets that will stand the rigors of sweeping willows and the occasional stream dip. The best source for quality collecting gear is BioQuip, 2321 Gladwick St., Rancho Dominguez, CA 90220. You may also want to check with Wildco, 95 Botsford Place, Buffalo NY 14216, or Forestry Suppliers, P.O. Box 8397, Jackson, MS 39284.

Clear, widemouthed plastic jars are great for bug collecting. Scrape out the peanut butter or whatever, and wash the jar thoroughly with warm, soapy water. Drill half a dozen holes through the lid, and replace the waxed cardboard insert with a piece of window screen. Finally, wad up a paper towel and shove it into the jar so your bugs will have something to cling to. Voilà!

Plastic jars are nice but sometimes can get squashed at the most unfortunate times. If the collecting jar is going to be knocked around in the back of a pickup truck or on the floor of a boat, consider using a coffee can or a heavy Nalgene bottle. Regardless of the type of jar you use, never, absolutely ever, leave it in the sun. Only a moment of exposure, even on a cool day, will turn your little friends into lint.

The six-pack is up to you. I'd suggest cans so you can squash the empties and carry them out in your back pocket.

Catching flying bugs is an art. In the morning and evenings, many of the insects are in flight and vulnerable to a quick whisk of your net. Mayflies and stoneflies are relatively slow of wing and even slower of wit; once they've entered the net, they're as good as gotten. Caddis, damsels, and dragonflies are amazingly deft and will often double back and out of the net. The trick with these speedsters is to twist the net handle as soon as the bugs make entry so they get trapped in the folds of netting.

During midday, the bugs will be hiding in the shade of stream or lakeside vegetation. The best bet is to sweep the net through the riparian growth. If you lack a pro-quality net, have a friend shake the willows and alders to flush the bugs into the open where you can bag 'em. Some bugs, such as stoneflies, will not fly out of the vegetation but will simply drop deeper into the growth. In this case, nothing

stonefly

The stonefly has four transparent wings that stack neatly atop its back.

beats going into the brush on your hands and knees with an aquarium net.

No matter how impressive the gear and innovative your technique, you *will* look like a dork prancing around the fields swishing a butterfly net. This is where the six-pack comes in. You may either numb yourself to the social ineptitude of it all or try to win over any spectators with an offer of a cold one. Don't be too surprised if they back away while politely declining your offer.

Do yourself a huge favor and don't try to identify your bugs in the field. Go back to your tent, motel room, or other comfortable and confined environment. If possible, put the bug jar in the refrigerator or ice chest for a few minutes to mellow out the hostages.

Here we go. Does your bug have tails? If so, are the wings

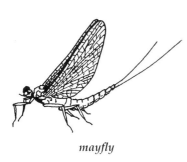

mayfly

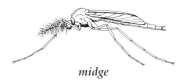

midge

The mayfly holds its wings like sails straight into the air.

folded neatly and flat atop its back? If you answered yes and yes again, you have identified a stonefly. These are found in every cool mountain stream and are important trout fare. If the bug has tails but the wings stick up in the air or out to the side, you have captured that loveliest of all insects, the famous mayfly.

The rest of your bugs do not have tails, right?

Look closely at the abdomen just behind where the wings are attached. See any fleshy or knobby protrusions? If so, this is a member of that vast family called Diptera. Diptera include true flies, mosquitoes, midges, and craneflies. Just be satisfied for now that you figured out it was a Diptera; we'll knock them down to size later.

Are the wings folded like a little pup tent over the back? If so, are they soft like moth wings or do they resemble cellophane? If they're soft, you're holding either a caddisfly or an aquatic moth. Look at its face. If it has a coiled tube dangling out from under its nose, it's a moth; you're looking at a mouthpart that can be uncoiled and extended deep within blossoms to reach nectar.

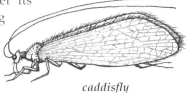

caddisfly

The caddisfly holds its mothlike wings over its back like a pup tent. If you see what looks like a caddisfly with coiled mouthparts hanging under its chin, it is an aquatic moth.

If your bug has soft, hairy, tent-shaped wings but lacks the coiled mouthpart, it is a caddisfly. Caddisflies range from almost too small to see to as big as your thumb. All are important to fish and fishermen.

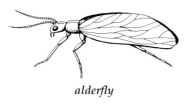

alderfly

dragonfly

Now, if those tent-shaped wings are crispy and like cellophane, your bug is most likely an alderfly. This fly has a thick, shiny head and well-developed mandibles. If it bit you with those gnarly jaws, you made a positive ID.

The remaining bugs do *not* have tails, do *not* have clubby protuberances behind their wings, and do *not* have their wings folded over their backs like a tent. The remainder of your aquatic insect adults should be long and slender, with relatively large compound eyes and crispy clear wings about as long as their bodies. If these wings stick out to the sides, you're looking at a dragonfly—but you knew that already. If these wings are folded together, above and parallel with the back, it's a damselfly.

The remaining bugs in your jar are most likely terrestrial insects; that is, they live their entire lives on land. This doesn't mean they are unimpor- tant to the angler. The

damselfly

mere fact that you caught them near water suggests that at one time or another, these guys might accidentally fall into the drink and become potential trout food. We'll discuss terrestrials later; for now you can put them in your garden.

Between this chapter and the previous one, you should be able to identify all the aquatic insects necessary to jump-start your career as an angling entomologist. You now have a stronger foundation from which to match the hatch than 85 percent of all the fly fishers out there. Believe it.

4

Taxonomy

The Rules of the Game

So far, we have broken the world of insects into two factions: those that undergo incomplete metamorphosis from egg, to nymph, to adult, and those that experience complete metamorphosis—egg, larva, pupa, adult.

Before we go further and actually play the game of identifying, describing, and mimicking the individual bugs, we need to lay down the rules of the game. These rules, the bane of every junior high school biology student, were devised by an obsessive-compulsive, probably sadomasochistic botanist in 1766.

Carl von Linné decided the natural world was a mess and he was going to fix it. From his, no doubt, immaculate garden in Sweden, he devised a hierarchical filing system that had a name and a place for every living thing on the planet. The system was far from perfect, but nothing better has been devised, possibly because no one else would be so sick as to try. Today an international panel of taxonomists and systematists tweaks the system by adding to and subtracting from the files as plants and animals and the taxonomic relationships to one another are discovered.

The rules of classification may seem intimidating at first, but in reality they are no more confusing than the menu at Denny's. When you belly up to the table, it's no great deal to distinguish between the plant and animal kingdoms: "Shall I eat a salad or real food?" Deciding that you want something that'll stick to the ribs, you swing with a meat dish and enter the kingdom of Animalia.

Craving meat, you'll next have to decide if you'll humor the wife by eating cod or go with your carnivorous lust and wolf down a slab of cow. In this fashion, you're making increasingly finite choices: "well done or raw," "salad or fries," "blue cheese or French," "for here or to go." In the end, you wind up with a meal that is unique unto itself and couldn't possibly be confused with any other. At this point, we can give it a scientific, or *binomial*, name, always written in italics. The first part of the scientific name is always capitalized and describes the meal in its generic (as in *genus*) form, and the second word describes the meal specifically (as in *species*). Note the clever emphasis on the roots of these words.

We might name our meal *Dennys cutteri*, and from now on you could go to any Denny's in the world, utter the words *Dennys cutteri*, and know you would be given a to-go bag filled with a rare sirloin and a green salad with two packets of lite blue cheese dressing. If by mistake the bag contained a side order of fries, you would have to give it a subspecies name (always lowercase and in italics): *Dennys cutteri spud*. Insects are just like that.

My simplified version of the hierarchical system works like this:

Taxon	Name (example)	Reason (excuse)
Kingdom	Animalia	It's not a plant
Phylum	Arthropoda	Has jointed legs
Class	Insecta	Has three body parts
Order	Plecoptera	All stoneflies
Family	Perlodidae	Some stoneflies
Genus	*Isoperla*	Little stoneflies
Species	*bilineata*	Little yellow stoneflies

There will be occasions when you'll see the taxons (groups of related organisms) further broken into infra-, super-, and sub-groups. The only time these might be relevant for fly fishing will be in the rare instance where one subspecies might vary a couple hook sizes from another subspecies. Other than that, ignore them.

As budding aquatic entomologists, you'll see that we're already at the class level (Insecta) in identifying insects, so the only taxons of interest to us are the order, family, genus, and species. Remember them.

What's in a name? Everything and nothing. If you were asked to tie patterns to represent the Michigan caddis, fishfly, sandfly, burrowing mayfly, and great olive-winged drake, how many flies would be in your box? One—*Hexagenia limbata* is the Latin name for all of these common names. It is most commonly known to anglers as the Hex.

Common names are sometimes descriptive—the blue-winged olive, for instance—but they're inevitably confusing. There are no fewer than thirteen different kinds of mayflies locally known as blue-winged olives.

Imagine that you're preparing for the trip of a lifetime, and you were told to bring a zillion blue-winged olives. Knowing that blue-winged olives were the size 12 bugs coming off the Truckee last summer (*flavilinea*), you fill the box appropriately. When you arrive at the Bighorn, you get skunked because the blue winged olives there happen to be size 22 (*Baetis*). "Oh, *those* blue-winged olives," you might sputter.

Scientific names are considered confusing and snobbish only because of tradition. Fly fishing is a centuries-old tradition unhampered by hundreds of years of progress, or so the purists might say. I'd like to remind them that gardening is an infinitely older tradition than fly fishing, yet we have no problem identifying our plants as petunias, begonias, and delphiniums. When was the last time you considered someone an uppity snob because he called a redwood tree a sequoia? Liberate yourselves from the stifling chains of tradition and start using some Latin and Greek.

Many people shun Latin because they're afraid of pronouncing the words wrong. Relax. It's a dead language, so even the pope can't dis you for pronouncing the words as you see fit. Commonly used pronunciations are as follows:

a	hat or uh
ae	bay or bee
ah	ball
ai	air
ay	lay
b	bass
c	cat
ch	crab or shoe
d	dog
e	wet
ee	we
ew	humor
f	fish
g	goat or ginger
h	hat
i	tin or, more commonly, spaghetti
j	jade
k	cow
l	lip
m	man
n	now
o	ox or hoe
oe	hoe
oo	room
p	pig
q	queer
r	rat
s	snake
t	trout
u	um or yule

v	Victor
w	wing
x	xylophone
y	wit or teeth
ye	wine
z	zebra

Here are a few examples:

Chironomid	kye-row-NO-mid *or* kye-ROH-no-mid
Baetis	BAY-tiss *or* BEE-tiss
Paraleptophlebia	pear-uh-lept-oh-FLEE-bee-uh
(I love this word)	
Hexagenia	hex-uh-GENE-ee-uh

And the favorite Latin word of all eighth-grade boys is the name for pine tree: *Pinus*. Go figure.

5

Bugs in the Kitchen
Grow Your Own

"Dad, what are these black things in my food?" I look at Lisa, Lisa looks at me, and Haley looks at both of us accusingly. All of us turn and look at the biggest of the bug tanks. The screen is open, and midges are swarming in a mating flight. Lisa and I scrape back our chairs and go over to watch, while Haley and Teal pick tiny insects off their applesauce. Having a few bugs in your food is a small price to pay for the joy and satisfaction of raising aquatic insects in the kitchen.

Every fly fisher should raise a few bugs. For less than the cost of a tank of gas, you can have a tank of bugs and host your very own hatch. I would suggest starting off with a "lake" tank. Lake-dwelling bugs are generally more temperature-tolerant and otherwise more durable than their fast-water brethren. Most pet shops sell starter tropical fish-tank kits that include a ten-gallon aquarium, filter, hood, and air pump for less than thirty bucks. Make sure you get an *undergravel* filter. The external type will quickly suck all of the bugs out of the water.

Set up the tank so that it gets bright light through a window but doesn't get hit with direct sun. Following the instructions in the aquarium kit, lay the plastic grid in the tank and insert the up-tubes and air stones. Cover the grid with a couple inches of coarse gravel, and then fill the tank with tap water. Turn on the air pump and allow the air stones to fizz overnight to neutralize any chlorine in the tap water. Chemicals can be purchased in any pet shop that will neutralize not only the chlorine, but any ammonia and heavy metals as well. Finally, put a handful of pond mud and a couple of goldfish in the tank, and let the whole thing stew for a couple weeks.

The goldfish poop and uneaten fish food will add nutrients to the tank, and the bacteria and tiny organisms in the mud will feed on the nutrients and colonize the gravel. A strong colony of bacteria is vital to keeping the nitrate levels in balance. Cutting corners at this step virtually guarantees that your bugs will live only a short and painful existence under your care.

After the two weeks are over, feed the goldfish to your cat, find them another home, or start a goldfish tank, if you've grown attached to them. In your bug habitat, they are of no use now.

While you are at the pet shop, study some of the aquatic plants that are for sale and chuckle at their ridiculously high cost. Go to your neighborhood pond and look at what grows in the water. Lo! Those are the same plants. Not only are these pond weeds free, but they come with free bugs, too.

Pull up a few of these weeds, keeping some of the roots and clinging mud intact, sweep a jelly strainer through the remaining aquatic veggies, and then put a generous handful of mud in your collecting bucket and see what critters are in it. Anything that swims, floats, burrows, or wriggles is fair game. Go home, dump all this stuff in your tank, and wait for the silt to clear.

You will be genuinely amazed at the density and diversity of bugs you collected. In anything like a normal pond, you will have sampled midge larvae, mayfly and damselfly nymphs, perhaps some caddisflies, and most certainly snails, scuds, and water beetles. If you're insanely lucky, you'll get a water scorpion . . . these little monsters have high entertainment value as they spear unsuspecting tadpoles and minnows, inject them with slow-acting poison, and then suck out their juices.

Even if they do so less operatically, all your bugs need to eat. *Spirulina* algae fish-food tabs will satisfy all the vegetarians in your keep, and the carnivores will take care of themselves. As the days go on, ecology does its thing, and you'll have fewer and fewer bugs. Your loss almost always will be because of the voracity of the damselfly nymphs. Damsel nymphs are cool, but their novelty quickly wears off when they are the only thing left in the tank. You will learn to thin their numbers out at the pond.

Another bug that loses its coolness is the *Siphlonurus* mayfly nymph. Unlike most mayflies, the *Siphlonurus* nymphs crawl to shore to molt into adults, rather than ascend to the water's surface. The *Siphlonurus*'s shoreward migration seems to be cued by light, and they aren't smart enough to figure out they can't get to the light through aquarium glass. The dumb little insects will bang their heads against the glass a few times, then attempt to molt on the bottom of the tank. It's best to get a basic entomology book or an angler's entomology such as *Mayflies*, by Malcolm Knopp and Robert Cormier, and learn to identify these guys, and then release them at the pond, rather than bring them home.

The snails and scuds will copulate in full view of an audience, and their numbers will grow dramatically. The damselflies will crawl out of the water on your air hoses—or better yet, on a few sticks you've jabbed into the gravel that are long enough to poke out of the water a few inches—and then molt into beautiful adults. Perhaps the best of all are the *Callibaetis* nymphs.

By placing a flood lamp above the tank, you can stimulate the nymphs to fill with gas and ascend to the surface to molt. In our fly-fishing classes, we try to have *Callibaetis* hatch on demand for our students. It is very cool!

A stream tank is a bit more challenging and a lot more expensive than a lake tank. Install the undergravel filters just as in the lake tank, but instead of air pumps, install jet pumps into each of the up-tubes. The pumps will suck water through the gravel, where bacteria cleans it, then squirt it back into the tank to create a flow. When arranged strategically, you can get these pumps to circulate the "stream" around the tank and between rocks where *Hydropsyche* caddisflies will spin nets to catch food.

The best way to populate the stream tank is to visit a nearby river with two or three five-gallon buckets. Partially fill the buckets with river water, and then add algae-coated rocks and rocks that have bugs attached to them. Roll rocks on the riverbed and hold a jelly strainer just downstream of them to catch dislodged critters. Sample both the fast water and the slow water, and sweep along undercuts and aquatic veggies to get a wide variety of insects.

Before you go home, pick out all the stonefly nymphs and release them. Most vegetarian stoneflies, such as the *Isogenus*, simply don't survive well in the average aquarium. The carnivorous stones, such as the *Calineuria*, will quickly eat every other bug in the tank before they start eating each other. If you find your bug population inexplicably thinning, it is likely a *Calineuria* slipped into the tank and is lurking under some dark rock.

You may or may not want to keep a crayfish or sculpin. Both do very well in stream aquariums but will feed on their neighbors if not kept satiated with earthworms and cat food. Crayfish can create a mess by digging burrows and leaving scraps of uneaten food about, but I think they're cute and worth the extra effort.

Along with spirulina tabs, add a small pinch of tropical fish flakes every two or three days. These flakes will get seined by the *Hydropsyche* caddis larvae and eaten with gusto.

Your stream tank will provide hours of wholesome entertainment for the entire neighborhood. You can invent games to play with your pets. A good one is to add bits of different-colored gravel to the aquarium so the caddisfly larvae will build paisley homes. Near the Fourth of July, you might want to offer them red, white, and blue.

Aquatic tanks are the next best thing to going underwater. You will gain an appreciation for the critters that dwell in that strange environment, and you will likely become a more careful wader. You (or your children) will acquire a taste for them as they land on your food, and who knows, you might even become a better angler.

6

Perception, Part I
Blood the Color of Money

The red-blood paradigm is so deeply ingrained in our psyche that when I glanced down at the green smoke billowing from my leg, it provoked nothing more than curiosity. Along with perpetually blown eardrums and body odor that smelled vaguely of off-gassing neoprene, bleeding green was just another exciting perk gained from working at a Monterey dive shop.

Color is not a concrete thing that can be held, kept in a box, or tied onto a hook. Color is a perception, and like all perceptions, its reality is described by the one doing the perceiving. Water is famous for filtering out color wavelengths. As you and a friend descend through water, your perception of blood being "blood" red will become iron red, then plum red, and finally stop being any kind of red at all. As you continue to descend, the color will morph through shades of purple, then brown, and ultimately into green. Your partner will describe the same color shifts, yet it is unlikely that he or she will perceive the colors exactly as you do. Because of minute differences in biochemical processing, anatomical structure, and neurological wiring, no two humans perceive colors precisely the same.

"What if your underwater partner were a fish?" you might ask. I would counter, "What if your underwater partner were a cow?" Knowing that no two humans see colors in exactly the same way, would you really expect a cow to see things exactly as you do? Of course not. Especially when it is swimming underwater. And, you'd better hope, a cow is much, much, much more closely related to your mother than is a trout.

A human's color perception spans violet, indigo, blue, green, yellow, orange, and red. A trout's color perception band is wider than a human's. Not only does it see all the colors we see, but it can also see a bit into the infrared and ultraviolet ranges.

Something has color because it absorbs all the (visible) light wavelengths except for those that express the color value you see. Black velvet absorbs all visible colors, so we perceive it as black— the absence of color. Elvis looks good painted on black velvet only because he is being contrasted with nothingness. Material that reflects all the (visible) light wavelengths appears white.

A green caddis larva looks green because it is absorbing all the visible wavelengths except for those between the blue and yellow frequencies. Caddis larva green is the blend of the reflected blue, green, and yellow spectrums of light. What if that larva also reflected the invisible ultraviolet frequencies? Would you know? No, that's why they're called invisible. Would a trout know? Probably yes, because they can see ultraviolet. What would you call the color a trout sees that might result from a caddis larva reflecting a blend of green and ultraviolet frequencies of light? Anything you want, just don't call it green.

Lots of money has been made by marketing "perfectly" colored flies and lures to anglers. One well-known entrepreneur, who is also a Ph.D. fisheries biologist and knows better, hucks a line of dubbing that supposedly matches each and every aquatic insect color. These colors match what *we* see, not what the fish sees.

The best way to make sure our fly presents the colors a trout is looking for is to blend a bunch of colors into the fabric of the imitation. Randall Kaufmann does exactly this with his highly effective Stimulators and stoneflies. Hold one of these gems up to the light and you'll notice that even though the general coloration might be orange or green, the dubbing contains fibers ranging from black to white and every color in between. Trout don't care if the wrong colors are there as long as the right colors are present. A lifetime ago, I described this behavior and coined the phrase "selective discrimination." The phrase has become part of angling vernacular, and I must admit to feeling a bit smug every time it crops up in some article.

Selective discrimination is what allows a trout to ignore the steel hook hanging out of a fly's butt yet refuse to eat the imitation because the perfectly shaped wing is a shade too opaque. Dave Whitlock took advantage of selective discrimination when he developed his Bright Dot series of flies. With the Bright Dots, he tied colorful chunks of yarn on the backs of otherwise perfectly normal flies. Anglers could easily identify their cheerful offerings bobbing amid the naturals, and it didn't bother the trout one whit.

Trout seem to prefer imitations that somewhat take on the color of their surroundings. Gary LaFontaine noticed that the same trout in the same run preferred Trudes tied with green wings when their background was the green of spring- and summertime alders and willows. In the fall, as the background foliage turned with the seasons, the trout preferred the same bugs with yellow or orange wings.

Brian Clarke and John Goddard, in their masterpiece, *The Trout and the Fly* (in my mind the most important piece of angling literature ever produced), note that spinners tied with orange wings outfished their clear-winged counterparts when the setting sun was casting its orange glow on the water. Midday, the orange-winged spinners failed miserably.

Now that you've read some one thousand words about the theory of color and trout fishing, let me clue you in to a little secret. It's all bunk. . . . Well, most of it anyway. I usually fish light patterns and dark patterns. I think proper value rather than color is what concerns most trout most of the time. Value is simply the shade of gray a fly would appear if seen in a black and white photograph. When looking at a fly, think in terms of Plus X rather than Kodachrome. Early and late in the season, bugs tend to be dark to enhance solar thermal gain. In midseason, they tend to be lighter to reflect desiccating heat. Put your power of reasoning to use here.

Sometimes contrasting values or colors can spark a trout's urge to bite. Black flies fished against the contrast of an evening sky can be deadly. (In case you were wondering, from underwater an evening sky looks silver, not black.) A dark body hovering in a puddle of silver light can prove irresistible. This is exactly what a fish sees when swimming underneath an E/C caddis. The parachute hackle rides on the film, where its weight bends the water into a concave, light-catching lens. The dark body of the fly floats in the middle of this silver dimple, silently crying to all who might hear, "Eat me!"

Simple strips of contrasting rabbit fur tied on a hook can produce devastating results in dim light or murky water. For this reason, the Goblin is my go-to fly early in the season when the water is discolored from runoff. As it pulses through light water, the black strip stands out like a beetle on a snowbank. When the Goblin darts into the shadows or swims against a dark background, the bright orange or white strip almost glows in contrast. Into the shadows and out again, the streamer literally turns on and off like something alive. Trout like that in a fly, regardless of color.

7

Perception, Part II
How Big Is Too Small?

Your ex-wife is right, size *does* matter.

Scientists will tell you that a trout's vision is somewhat less acute than a human's. How they know that, I can't tell, but I can tell you that in a fish's world, a trout sees much better than we do. Hundreds, perhaps thousands, of times I have finned in the water just behind a trout and watched as it cocked its fins, flared its tail, and raised its nose in eager anticipation of an approaching morsel of food. It is a body language common to all trout in all waters across the world. Just as a dog cocks its head, lifts its eyebrows, raises its ears, and wags its tail when you open a can of puppy chow, a trout gets perky in its own special way when it spies a piece of food.

Rarely do I see the food item drifting toward us before the trout sees it. Invariably it is the fish's behavior that alerts me to the item. Many, many, many times I can't see the item until it is inches from the trout's nose, and far too many times to count, I'm unable to figure out what the trout saw at all. From several feet away, trout can see Daphnia and copepods and mayfly egg masses the size of the period at the end of this sentence. They see, or otherwise perceive, these minute flecks against a swirling background of bubbles, swaying vegetation, and drifting debris. I don't have a clue how they do it.

When your nymph drifts several inches past an unmotivated trout, don't assuage your ego by thinking she didn't see it. She saw it all right; she was simply unimpressed with what you had to offer. It is quite possible that in this instance, size did matter and you simply didn't cut the mustard. How does your ego feel now?

Nine out of ten people use a fly that is too big. Three reasons: It is easier to get the tippet through the eye of the fly; it is easier to see on the water; and to us, live flies simply appear larger than they really are. If these are the reasons you choose to use flies that are bigger than the naturals, that is fine—at least you have reasons. Some people don't have any reason other than that it was a cool-looking fly in the box.

How do you know what size is the right size? A good place to start is by catching a natural bug. Kind of like the trout before you set it next to a tape measure, bugs on the wing invariably look bigger than they are. A size 12 pale morning dun rising and falling in a mating flight backlit by the setting sun will quickly shrink to a size 14 or even 16 when it gets pinched between your thumb and forefinger.

What if several kinds of bugs are out and about? Imitate the size of the most numerous species, not the biggest. Sometimes the most famous hatches create the most famous disappointments. There is nothing quite so humbling as traveling to the Fall River to fish the Hex hatch, or going to the Upper Sac to meet the golden stones, or even visiting the Truckee to experience its green drakes, only to find that the trout are swimming around these giant morsels to sip the scads of little stuff on the water. Not one angler in a hundred will happily accept the obvious. It is the reason I quit being a fishing guide.

I'll never forget the frustration of dealing with a client (we'll call him Mortimer) who came to the Truckee expressly to fish the green drake hatch. Two years previously, he had directed me to phone him when the green drakes were on. When the hatch started, I gave him a call, and he immediately closed up shop in Davis and ran up the mountain. That night we were on the water.

It was one of those rare Sierra evenings when the air was warm and viscous. You could actually feel its softness against your skin. A buttery moon was rising over Mount Rose, the nighthawks were screaming in the purple sky, and green drakes were fluttering everywhere. Unfortunately for Mort, instead of blasting the fat size 10 mayflies, the trout were sipping spinners from a heavy *tibialis* fall. Mort was beside himself with frustration. No matter how many times I offered him a rod rigged with a spinner, he refused and kept tying on various green drake imitations. Though it was a magic summer night on the water, he couldn't see it; he was mad at the world, mad at his equipment, mad at the fish, but mostly mad at me because I couldn't make the trout eat his fly. He had taken one of the finest nights of the season and turned it into a miserable experience.

If the streamside cobwebs are littered with size 16 bugs from yesterday's hatch, what size nymph would you expect might be an appropriate one? You're right, a size 14. Remember that the mayfly, caddisfly, or stonefly adult in the spiderweb had to fit neatly inside the skin of its former aquatic self. Fishing a hatch simplifies the size dilemma. The adult might be a size 16 and the nymph a 14, but in their combined state of emergence, the size might be a 10 or even an 8. Size is rarely an issue when fishing emergers, because trout see the hatchlings ranging from nymphs with bulging wing pads to almost fully escaped adults with only the tips of the abdomens still in the nymphal exuviae.

Probably a better idea than looking into spiderwebs to figure out what size nymph to use would be to actually get your sleeves wet and pull a few rocks out of the river. Early in the season, you will likely find a plethora of aquatic insects in a dizzying array of shapes and sizes. I would suggest picking a nymph that approxi-mates the size of the average bug on the rock. If the water is murky, you might bump it up a size to make it easier for the fish to see.

Midsummer is the time when you will find the least number of bugs on your rock. The vast majority of the bugs hatched ear-lier in the season, and in their wake will be their planktonic off-spring. The bugs you do see will likely be fall-hatching caddis or those species that live for two or more years. All will probably be pretty big. As a rule, in midsummer I use large imitations when blindly searching the water. Not only are most of the aquatics big then, but crayfish and grasshoppers are also on the menu.

The fall can be tricky. Crayfish and the multiyear stoneflies will still be on your rock, but those planktonic larvae and nymphs will now be visible and available by the zillions. They might be too small to imitate with a fly, but they are easily big enough for trout to strain with their gill rakers. Often fall trout will have stomachs bulging with green curd. This is not mint jelly, but a coagulated mass of tiny macroinvertebrates. Unless you are fortunate enough to be working a midge or blue-winged olive hatch, fish big imitations, because you have no other choice.

Throughout the winter, the micro macros will grow into big macros, and come spring, you will once again have a limitless number of bug sizes to choose from.

8

Upslope Blow-In

Lost Lake didn't want to be found.

Deep inside the avalanche chute, Lisa and I climbed skyward. We twisted and wound our way around truck-size granite boulders and plunged through tangles of downed trees. Far above us, rotting snowfields sent unannounced volleys of rocks that skipped and whined past us leaving plumes of dust and the tang of ozone in their wake.

We finally reached the safety of the snow line and trudged eastward and ever upward toward the basin where we thought Lost Lake should be. The basin was nothing more than a hanging valley through which a series of small creeks trickled among patches of snow. We climbed over the ridgeline to the next basin and then a third; the lake was not there.

Lost Lake is one of those hallowed spots that don't appear on the USGS topographic maps. Its location is protected by the few who have found it, and the photos of the exceedingly large golden trout caught and released from its waters only add to its sacred, almost mystical reputation.

We climbed atop a huge boulder and enjoyed a leisurely lunch of dried apricots, cheddar cheese, M&Ms, and icy water spiked with crushed peppermint leaves. While we ate, flocks of gray-crowned rosy finches fluttered over the snow patches like noisy children. Seemingly out of nowhere, a pair of ptarmigan waddled through the heather and began pecking and scratching at the snowfields occupied by the finches.

The afternoon breeze stiffened and chilled us in our sweat-dampened clothes. We decided to throw in the towel and head back to camp some four miles and three thousand vertical feet below us. On a hunch, we climbed toward a notch in the granite-studded skyline in hopes that it would provide us with a means to circumvent the nasty avalanche chute. At the base of the notch, nestled in a picture-perfect setting of white granite, blue skies, and green heather, lay Lost Lake. To make the picture even better, trout—large ones—were breaking the surface in slow, deliberate rises.

Carefully, we worked our way through the talus field to the downwind shore of the lake so that we could punch our casts directly into the wind. We chose to fight the wind on the cast; our payoff would be that the wind would drift our flies back toward us, assuring long, drag-free drifts. We strung up the rods and tied on small midge emergers—the default choice for free-rising timberline trout when no insects are visible.

Despite the wind, we were able to lay out passable casts between the gusts. The tiny emerger patterns slowly bobbed their way back to us through the chop. We punched out cast after cast, and as often as not, trout would rise within inches of our flies but always ignored them completely.

While I continued to flail, Lisa wandered to a sheltered cove and then kneeled to pick something from the water. Staring into her cupped hand, she called out, "You won't believe this. . . ."

After a long, teasing pause, I finally relented and shouted back, "Okay, what won't I believe?"

"This lake is full of *infrequens*!"

Ephemerella infrequens, better known as pale morning duns or more simply PMDs, live in rich streams and rivers. We were close to twelve thousand feet at a nearly sterile lake. I shouted into the wind, "You're right. I don't believe it."

Lisa quickly replaced her fly and in a single cast was fast to a big, fat golden trout that was going berserk. In amazement I asked her, "What are you using?"

She grinned. "You wouldn't believe it!"

I started picking through the flotsam that had collected against the rocky shore. It was full of carpenter ants, small beetles, grasshoppers, caddisflies, and hundreds of waterlogged PMDs. None of these insects lived within a dozen miles of where we fished. The chunky goldens in this timberline tarn were feeding courtesy of a phenomenon known as upslope blow-in.

Upslope blow-in is the sole reason that many otherwise barren Sierra (and other mountain range) lakes support trout fish-

The stark high country has little ability to produce much in the way of food. Its ecosystem largely depends on the windborne nutrients from productive lands thousands of feet below.

eries. As the air warms in California's Central Valley and Nevada's Great Basin, it rises. As it ascends, it carries with it a payload of thousands if not millions of lowland insects. The bug-filled breezes travel high into the Sierra, where they deposit their bounty onto the stark landscape. Not only trout, but also birds, lizards, frogs, and other residents of the high Sierra depend on the daily feast.

Trout are so accustomed to the afternoon windfall that they expect to see a cornucopia of bugs dropping onto their watery domain. Oblige them with a fly of your own. My favorite upslope blow-in pattern is a size 14 tan Elk Hair Caddis. The Elk Hair Caddis looks like so many kinds of trout food that it doesn't really matter if the meal of the day is leafhopper, grasshopper, moth, or small stonefly; the imitation will fool the average trout I hang out with. If the valley streams are experiencing a caddis hatch and the upslope winds have captured a few thousand of those hapless critters, the Elk Hair Caddis will work just fine then as well.

Upslope blow-in is the reason I tend to bring a stiffer rod than many people into the high country. More than a few times, I've been forced to cast large Stimulators and Madam Xs into a hard wind to imitate the hoppers and butterflies imported by upslope blow-in. A 5-weight rod will be a club on the smaller Sierra waters, but when upslope blow-in is calling, I appreciate the backbone.

9

All That Glitters

Most aquatic insects create or trap bubbles of gas at some time in their lives. They use these bubbles for respiration, buoyancy, and as an aid for escaping the subadult form. Whatever reason these insects use bubbles, all reveal themselves to trout as dazzling, quicksilver images that appear to glow with an inner light. Bubble-encrusted insects look like living jewels.

Bubble-encased bugs are extremely visible underwater, and trout often swim right past other food items to snare a glittering insect. Many times trout will key in on and feed *only* on sparkling insects. When the time is right, bubbles trigger takes. It's as simple as that. Beads, reflective plastics, and multilobed fabrics have been used to imitate aquatic air-encrusted insects. As good as these materials are, they fall far short of how good they *should* be. Hundreds of hours spent diving in both lakes and streams observing trout feed has convinced me that bubbles are simply too important to imitate; they must be captured.

The best way to make bubbles cling to flies is to do what living insects do. Bubble-capturing insects are covered with thousands of wax-coated unwettable hairs that actually repel water from the body.

The first time I rubbed beeswax into a hare's ear and tossed it in the water, I knew I'd found the answer. The nymph glittered like a diamond, and the buoyancy of the air crust caused the bug to swim and drift in the current like a creature come to life. It was too easy.

After ten years of refining these "glitter bugs" and testing them under a myriad of conditions, I've drawn some pretty pat conclusions:

- First of all, they work. When shimmering insects are active, these "glitter bugs" outfish any other pattern. I've repeatedly observed sophisticated trout pull off their feeding lanes to chase down air-encrusted nymph patterns.
- The best bubble-trapping nymph/pupa/boatman patterns are the LaFontaine Sparkle Pupa tied with wool rather than Antron and the Bird's Nest. Both the Bird's Nest and the Sparkle Pupa have an overbody that acts as a cage that

A Bird's Nest nymph that has been rubbed with powdered fly floatant creates a bubble that makes it deadly effective when imitating glittering insects.

holds the bubble against the body of the fly. The *Baetis* spinner requires its own simple pattern.

- "Glitter bug" patterns are best tied with natural materials containing lots of fuzz or spike. Natural materials absorb floatant, and the coarse structure of the natural filaments help entrain bubbles. Slick synthetics do not absorb floatant and easily shed their bubbles in fast water or when slapped through the surface.

- The easiest way to apply bubbles is to treat your nymph like a dry fly. Shake it vigorously in fly desiccant powder such as Shimazaki's Shake or Frog's Fanny. Even better is to actually scrub the desiccant into the nymph fibers. Stay away from other products. Liquid floatants don't last long and make the fly sticky. Paste, grease, and wax products mat the hairs, resulting in a loss of bubble-grabbing potential.

- Dry the nymph between drifts with false casts. When the bug becomes waterlogged, re-treat it with a desiccant fly floatant.

- Do not weight the fly itself. Allow the buoyancy of the trapped air to "swim" the fly naturally in the current. Use split shot a few inches up the leader to take the bug to the desired depth.

Thanks to the work of Gary LaFontaine, caddisflies are probably the best known of the glittering bugs. Some caddisfly larvae capture bubbles of air and hitch rides with the currents. I've watched both *Brachycentrus* and *Amiocentrus* caddis larvae drifting, often in large numbers, with a single small bubble clutched within their legs. In our fly-fishing school's "bug tank," an eight-foot, three-hundred-gallon aquarium recirculated at four thousand gallons an hour by half a dozen pumps, we've had shoals of *Brachycentrus* bobbing around the current on bubbles they've harvested from fizzing air stones.

A caddisfly pupa swims to the surface to emerge. Its ascent is aided by two bright bubbles that have formed under its thorax.

Caddis pupae sometimes generate bubbles within the pupal sheath as they prepare to "hatch" into the adult form. These bubbles can appear anywhere on the bug but are most common on the dorsal aspect just behind the head. The pupae are erratic but very strong swimmers, and the imitation is best presented with an active twitchy retrieve or a down-and-across-stream swing.

Most of the students in our school seem to be aware that at least some caddis pupae generate bubbles during emergence; however, in my experience, the egg-laying adults are *far* more dramatic and enticing to trout.

Many caddisfly adults lay their eggs subsurface. Lacking gills, they must transport their air supply underwater with them. The entire insect becomes encased in an incredible shimmering sheath of air, which allows it to labor underwater for extended periods. This bubble, called a *plastron*, absorbs oxygen from the surrounding water as the insect breathes from its store. (Ovipositing aquatic moths do the same.)

Ovipositing caddis swim in very smooth and swift fashion . . . a down-and-across-stream swing is a perfect presentation. When a major ovipositing is taking place, trout often ignore swimming

An adult caddisfly swims underwater to lay its eggs. Above water, it looks like a plain brown bug, but underwater, encased in a shroud of bubbles, it sparkles like a diamond.

caddis and simply graze on the myriad of bugs clambering over the riverbed. I've watched trout even pluck empty bubbles trapped under and against rocks and logs. The best presentation in this situation is a drag-free drift of an air-coated nymph right along the riverbed.

At least a few emerging midge pupae fill their pupal sheaths with gas. Unlike caddis, they do not actively swim but simply drift and squirm as they are buoyed to the surface. When viewed from below, blood midge pupae look like orange sparks drifting from a campfire. A Brassie is an excellent imitation, as is a simple tuft of orange squirrel dubbing treated with powdered fly floatant. These are deadly when drifted under a long, light leader (use split shot to keep the air shells from floating them on the surface).

Mayfly nymphs fill their exoskeletons with gas to aid in emergence. I've watched *Callibaetis* and numerous *Ephemerella* hang in the surface film aided by the buoyancy of their gas-filled exoskeletons. When viewed from above, they appear quite normal. From an underwater vantage, these emergers glow golden, particularly around the edges as sunlight reflects from their taut bodies. When the nymph pops open, the exoskeleton relaxes, loses its shine, then quickly assumes a shimmering glow as the adult pulls free from its translucent, frequently bubble-filled nymphal husk.

One of the most amazing yet underutilized "glitter bugs" is the *Baetis* spinner. Many *Baetis* mayflies are unique in that the adult females (spinners) crawl underwater and affix their eggs to streambed structure. For some reason, although mating occurs above water, the females are often joined underwater by males. These mayflies each trap a bubble of air between their upright wings and look like tiny angels as they roam about the streambed. For more information on *Baetis* spinners, see chapter 16.

Ovipositing *Baetis* are easy to imitate. They can be fished dead drift anywhere in the water column but are most effective along the streambed.

In waters with back swimmers and water boatmen, glitter-bugs will work anytime, because these plastron-carrying insects are seen by trout every day all season long. In other waters, "glitter bugs" are most effective during emergence or egg laying. When insects are found entering or leaving the water, it's a good bet trout are seeing diamonds before their eyes and your air-bejeweled fly is a sight for sore lips.

PART TWO

The Menu

10
Ants

For over 50 million years ants have been the overwhelmingly dominant insect everywhere on land outside the polar and arctic ice fields. By my estimate, between 1 and 10 million billion individuals are alive at any moment, all of them together weighing, to the nearest order of magnitude, as much as the totality of human beings.

—Edward O. Wilson, *Naturalist*

Ants are the most numerous insects on earth and as such are the terrestrial insect most frequently encountered by trout. Ants can be successfully fished all season long but are at their best during "migrations," when millions of the creatures cloud the air and boil the water.

Borne on temporary wings, these weak fliers spew from their colonies like glistening smoke in search of suitable habitat in which to establish new colonies. Before that habitat is found,

A carpenter ant excavating tunnels into a log. Carpenter ants can approach an inch in length and swarm in the thousands, creating feeding frenzies when they fall on the water.

however, nearly all of the ants will have succumbed to the gnashing jaws of Mother Nature and human invention. Frequently the first sign of an ant migration is the distinctive patter of hapless bodies being dashed against your windshield. Ant swarms are often detected by the sight of wheeling birds and the sound of their raucous cries as they gorge on the tangy bugs.

Weather also plays an important role in the destiny of ants. A sudden cold snap will kill untold millions, and wind and rain can beat them to the earth or drive them to inhospitable environs. One of these environs is trout water.

Upslope blow-in is a phenomenon where warm valley winds laden with insects rise into the mountains and deposit their burdens into the high country. Ant swarms often get trapped in these thermal upwellings and become food for winter-starved trout many dozens of miles away. It is such a predictable phenomenon that ant patterns are at the top of my list as "must-have" high-country fly patterns.

The majority of ant swarms occur during the first truly hot days of summer. Coincidentally, this is also the time termites are in flight. Ants typically swarm during the day and termites at dusk, and trout love 'em both. Ant patterns also work perfectly as termite imitations.

The absolute best waters for anting are those bordered by dead trees. Beavers and the Army Corps of Engineers are notorious for drowning stands of trees and creating ant factories adjacent to hungry trout. Trout are so used to eating ants that they willingly consume them all season long. Observant anglers since the Vince Marinaro days have observed that trout actually seem to prefer ants over other morsels when a multiplicity of food items are available.

Trout go crazy over ants but seldom seem greatly impressed with ant patterns. Ant patterns that look cool in the fly box rarely work as well as they seem like they should. The answer is in front of your eyes . . . if you go underwater.

Real ants are covered with minute bristles that have a tendency to trap numerous small bubbles of air. An ant that looks black from our vantage point very often is sparkly silver from a trout's view. Typical ant patterns simply look dead in the water.

Foam ants look very good because the tiny pockets in the foam hold glistening bubbles. Unfortunately, foam ants tend to be high floaters whereas real ants are low floaters and sink rapidly.

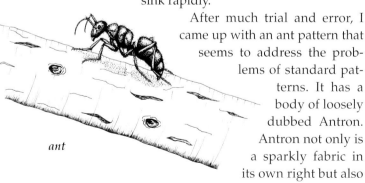

ant

After much trial and error, I came up with an ant pattern that seems to address the problems of standard patterns. It has a body of loosely dubbed Antron. Antron not only is a sparkly fabric in its own right but also has a multilobed cross section that tends to trap bubbles. The top half of the ant is a deer-hair "shell" tied on in Humpy style. The deer hair looks nice, but much more important, its hollow-celled interior helps float the ant pattern in the film. The tips of the deer hair are posted upright, around which a few turns of hackle are wrapped parachute-style. The para hackle helps hold the ant in the film and dents the water identically to the dent made by the legs (and wings, if present) of the natural.

Knowing full well an imitation will never be close to perfect, I named the pattern the Perfect Ant after the tremendous amount of trial and error that went into its design. As they say, practice makes perfect.

Unlike mayflies, which drift downcurrent like little clones of one another, ants present themselves in all sorts of contorted forms, so exact size imitation is rarely necessary. Most people tend to fish ants that are too small. In the Sierra, where carpenter ants abound, a size 10 is not too large and can act as a cross pattern for trout accustomed to eating beetles.

Fishing an ant pattern is pretty straightforward. Get a good, clean, drag-free drift, and the fly will probably be consumed. If the pattern sinks, so much the better. Ants are terrestrial insects, poorly adapted to being in the water, and they drown quickly. Repeatedly I've watched trout let live ants drift past in the overhead film and key in on those ants that had drowned and were being served at nose level. If your ant doesn't seem to work as well as it should as a dry, bite a piece of split shot onto the leader and fish it like a nymph under an almost taut line. Trout will hate you for it.

11

Aquatic Moths
The Other Caddisflies

The insects were in full offensive attack mode; their silver streaks blurred past me like quicksilver bullets. They crawled over my face, my hair, and my hands. They swam up my shorts and laid their eggs on my inner thighs. They loved me like a rock.

I was in the Truckee River in the midst of a swarm of *Petrophila truckeealis*. Very few sizable insects in any trout stream mass in these concentrations. The larvae that transform into *P. truckeealis* can dwell on riverbed boulders in densities of up to forty individuals per square foot. On some rivers in the Rockies, the rocks are so slippery with moth casings that they are a hazard to wading. Unlike mayflies, which live for only a single day after hatching, and caddisflies, which might live a few

aquatic moth

The web covering the aquatic moth caterpillar is rimmed with holes to allow water to pass through. These webs, usually mistaken for globs of algae, can number in the hundreds on a single boulder.

weeks, these bugs evolve into winged adults that live in excess of two months. The terrestrial form feeds on nectar and returns frequently to the river to lap moisture. These bugs are a fly fisherman's dream . . . but wait, there's more! Not only do these insects live in insane numbers and for months at a time, but they also can cycle through three hatches per season.

P. truckeealis is a moth—an aquatic moth. Its eggs are laid on the underside of floating leaves, on and in aquatic plants, but most commonly are deposited on rocks deep underwater. The eggs hatch within a couple of weeks and produce tiny caterpillars.

The larva looks pretty much like a typical terrestrial caterpillar: The thorax has three pairs of legs, distinguishing it from beetle larvae, and the abdomen sports pairs of short prolegs, distinguishing it from aquatic fly larvae. The *P. truckeealis* caterpillar lives its entire life underwater and breathes through the numerous gills that adorn its succulent body.

The newborn caterpillar quickly finds a dent or divot in a rock and creates a refuge by spinning a flat, scablike web over the top of the rugosity. The larva artfully cuts small holes in the silk that direct water into and through the dwelling. These scabs soon become impregnated with algae and turn to yellowish or rust-colored blemishes. Despite the fact that any given boulder might harbor many hundreds of these highly visible scabs, they remain ignored by all but the most observant angler.

Under the silk covering, the caterpillar dines on algae and diatoms until it morphs into the pupal form. Prior to pupation, the larva cuts a semicircular escape hatch in the silken covering. At the end of the abdomen of the pupa are hooks that attach permanently to the silk. After approximately a month of pupation, the puparium opens and the moth emerges. The moth pulls itself through the escape slit and crawls, swims, or floats to the surface. This emergence normally occurs at last light and into the night, and even though trout gorge on the feast, by now most anglers are back at the truck peeling their waders or have already made a beeline for the bar. To fish the nocturnal aquatic moth emergence, patience is a virtue. (As a side note: Like most moths, these guys are attracted to light. Turn on your vehicle's headlamps while dressing down from a day on the water. You will find not only a collection of moths, but also caddisflies, mayflies, and a dead battery.)

The adult moth lives up to two months, and for some reason the female often lives twice as long as the male. The moths feed on plant nectar and remain close to the river. They are frequently encountered by anglers, who tend to dismiss them as everyday caddisflies. Like a caddisfly, this moth holds its wings in a pup-tent configuration over its back. The forewing is a drab buff color, but the hind wing is decorated with intricate patterns. The streamside diagnosis between the aquatic moth and the caddisfly is that the moth holds a mouth siphon coiled under its nose; the caddis has no proboscis.

The sex life of these moths is wonderful. The female releases a pheromone that attracts males from great distances. Once the male hunts down the attractive scent source and the willing female therein, foreplay commences. The male approaches the

An aquatic moth affixing eggs to a midstream boulder. In the hand, the moth is pale gray, but underwater, it appears to be brilliant white as a result of the air trapped in the fibers of its wings.

female and gently taps her abdomen with his palps. He taps and caresses until the babe is aroused, and then they mate and mate and mate. Over and again. Repeatedly, over a period of hours. Once mating is over, the female limps away from her suitor and flies upstream for a considerable distance. This upstream winged migration is necessary to assure that the entire moth population doesn't end up in the inhospitable lowlands as a result of downstream drift of the eggs or larvae.

At dusk the female swims to the bottom of the river to lay her eggs in the rocky substrate. She has no gills and must carry oxygen with her in the form of air bubbles clinging to her body. She holds her air-cloaked, tent-shaped wings tight against her body and slips through the water like a thick silver needle. Specialized hairs on her legs act as paddles; the moth is an amazingly strong swimmer.

Considering that these moths live by the thousands, return to the water repeatedly, and can have up to three hatches in a year, it is amazing that there is not a single imitation that specifically mimics this creature.

A size 12 to 16 Bird's Nest coated in a desiccant powder such as Shimazaki's Shake closely imitates the natural. Cast the fly down and across stream, and retrieve it close to the riverbed in short, quick strips. Many of the moths get beaten up by the rigors of ovipositing and never return to shore. The bodies, sometimes dozens of them, collect in eddies and backwaters. Trout gorge on the fallen moths with gluttonous abandon, and a dead-drifted soft-hackle (I like partridge and orange) can prove deadly.

12

Back Swimmers and Boatmen

Silver flashes reflect off the glass of the scuba mask. If I turn just a little, the scintillations tickle my peripheral vision and my eyes reflexively jerk toward them. The sparks are hard to ignore.

Rolling onto my back, I watch the abstract flashes turn into silver bullets reigning terror in the otherwise pastoral setting of the trout pond.

Back swimmers hold silently in the film, their tails breaking the surface to feed on fresh air. The black compound eyes look painted on, uncomfortably similar to those of the Roswell aliens. The unblinking eyes survey the domain beneath them, searching for predators and prey. I wonder into which category I've been filed.

A small water beetle scuttles amid the sedge roots, and a back swimmer breaks off the film like a falcon from the clouds.

A water boatman refreshes its air supply while surveying the terrain below for potential victims.

With three powerful strokes of its paddle-shaped legs, the swimmer reaches the bottom of the pond in pursuit of the beetle.

The beetle scurries clockwise around the roots as it senses its impending demise. The back swimmer is not easily dissuaded. Its right paddle is held aloft while the left one strokes, and the swimmer pirouettes right and vectors in for the kill. At the moment of contact, a pair of raptorial claws unfold beneath the swimmer's chin and engage the hapless beetle in their spiny grasp. Immediately, the razor-sharp beak of the swimmer pierces the soft connective tissues between the beetle's head and thorax. As digestive juices are pumped into the dying beetle, the back swimmer and its prey are buoyed gently to the surface by the swimmer's glistening packet of air.

Back swimmers and water boatmen are members of the order Hemiptera. The most noticeable difference between the two is that water boatmen swim on their tummies and back swimmers don't. On closer inspection, the back swimmers have a segmented, sharply pointed beak admirably suited for piercing

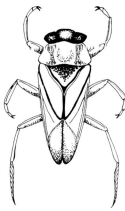

back swimmer

the bodies of their prey. Water boatmen, being not strictly carnivores, have a kinder, gentler rounded beak. Both bugs can and will, however, draw blood from the relatively soft flesh of a human being.

Humans have been known to bite back. In Mexico, toasted back swimmers, called ahuautle, are eaten like pumpkin seeds, and in Asia, both back swimmers and boatmen are considered delicacies. In the States, we are content to use the dried and ground-up bugs as turtle and aquarium fish food. Trout also know that boatmen and back swimmers taste good. In fact, they taste so good that at times fish will feed on them to the exclusion of all else.

One of the more perplexing hatches I've ever encountered was at a fertile lake in eastern Oregon. The water was boiling with trout. The grabs were splashy, and some truly huge fish were leaving toilet bowl swirls. Amid all the trout, the water was getting pocked and dimpled as if we were in a hailstorm. I was smart enough to know that under the cloudless autumn skies, we weren't experiencing hail, but I wasn't smart enough to have brought a seine out in the boat.

For a frustrating hour and a half, we flailed and failed in our attempts to seduce a fish. We tried every kind of nymph, streamer, emerger, and dry fly in our box. The only thing we apparently didn't try was the fly that might work. It was almost a relief when the rise finally stopped and we could go back to camp.

On the row home, a lone fish sucked in the trolled leech and told us the tale. Its belly was distended as if the trout had eaten a hardball. Pine nut–size back swimmers, many still flipping wildly, spilled out of its mouth. The mystery was solved, and as with most mysteries, the answer should have been obvious all along. The hail was actually a blitz of migrating back swimmers.

A brilliant silver capsule of air, the plastron, is far and away the feature of the back swimmer that trout most key in on. Many fly tiers ignore the quicksilver effect but take great pains to imitate the back swimmer's legs, which feeding fish hardly notice.

Both back swimmers and boatmen are strong fliers and will travel great distances to redistribute themselves. Their affinity for bright light and shimmering bodies of water makes suburban swimming pools equipped with underwater lamps irresistible targets of their affection. Once located in a new water, the male boatmen will make lurid song by scratching their rasping legs against the sides of their faces. Their presence, thus announced, presumably establishes territory and seduces lusty water boatwomen.

The next evening, the "hail" started to fall once again, and once again the surface came alive. We took light brown Bird's Nests, rubbed them in dry-fly floatant powder, and fed them to the trout. A small split shot was required to keep the buoyant nymphs submerged as we swam them to the boat. It was a journey the nymphs seldom made without getting clobbered.

Both back swimmers and water boatmen breathe oxygen from a bubble they carry with them. This bubble, called a *plastron*, clings tightly to a dense pad of unwettable hairs on the bug's abdomen. A second, lesser bubble is carried between the body and wings. From above, these drab insects look like drab insects; from underwater, however, these bubble-encrusted beasts glisten like jewels.

Unlike trout, many anglers key in on the oarlike legs of the back swimmers, going to great effort to replicate these structures.

Trout are generally unimpressed with the anglers' efforts and much prefer to eat any old generic nymph that sparkles or, better yet, carries a bubble of air.

A Bird's Nest rubbed in powdered floatant is about as close a clone as you'll ever find in the world of insect imitations. The floatant keeps the Bird's Nest in the film. A small split shot a few inches down the leader won't be enough weight to submerge the Nest, but it *will* be enough to pull the head under so the fly rests canted in the water just like the natural does as it gathers surface air.

A sharp tug on the fly line will cause the Nest to dive, and an erratic retrieve gives a pretty darn good rendition of a back swimmer jinking about. Pause and give the line some slack, and the air-encrusted nymph drifts back to the surface for another breath of fresh air. Perfect.

13
Baitfish

A few springs back, Lisa and I were fishing the Marquesas when we heard, then saw, hundreds of large animals bursting out of, then crashing back into, the warm tropical sea. Being cold-blooded sports from California, our first impression was that this was an unbelievably huge pod of sea lions rolling up the coast. As the leaping forms got closer, we realized they weren't sea lions at all, but tarpon. A massive hammerhead shark was sawing back and forth through the school, and tarpon the size of rottweilers were spraying from the water like shad fleeing a bass. The melee ended in a geyser of brilliant blood and a shower of glistening scales the size of hockey pucks. Such is the life of a baitfish.

A baitfish is any fish small enough to be eaten by a larger fish. This might be a fish of the same species or even the offspring of the consumer. At one time or another, all fish are baitfish. (*Forage fish* is the technically correct term, but *baitfish*, or just *bait*, is what most anglers use.)

The fine details of a baitfish imitation are of value only to the human observer. Fish key in on the basic shape, size, silhouette, and behavior of the prey.

Just as insects come in different shapes and enjoy various lifestyles, so do baitfish, and a variety of patterns and techniques must be employed if we are to successfully target piscivores. Dave Whitlock has divided forage fish into four groups for considering how to tackle an imitation. (For a complete dissertation on "matching the minnow," pick up a copy of his classic book, *Dave Whitlock's Guide to Aquatic Trout Foods*.) Here is a brief discussion of each of the four groups:

Group I. Schooling open-water baitfish. In fresh water, examples of Group I species are smelt and shad. Both are very shiny, thin, and horizontally compressed.

Regardless of the bait species, trout and bass hit schools in much the same way. They race through the school, relentlessly chasing a single individual fish, or they blitz the school and randomly slash at bait as they pass by. The marauders then return to eat the crippled and dying bait at their leisure.

To imitate the actions of a dying baitfish, use a pattern that flutters to the bottom, such as a Deceiver or Matuka. Simply cast the streamer into the school of bait and let it drop. Much more fun is to imitate the frantic action of a wounded baitfish attempting to escape. Nothing beats the jigging action of a Clouser Minnow. I like several hard strips followed by a drop. Often an erratic retrieve is more effective than a steady strip—pause, strip—pause. Work the edges of a school rather than casting directly into it when using a fleeing pattern.

Group II. Solitary or small group fish. Chubs, whitefish, trout, and dace are examples of common Group II species. Schools of young dace and chubs are frequently encountered in the backwaters along river edges and in the shallow bays of lakes. Marauding trout will make their presence known by their active pushes and V-shaped wakes, frequently preceded by showers of small fish. In these shallow conditions, flashy flies tend to spook the predators, and I usually use nothing more than a Bird's Nest nymph. Shape, size, and action are much more important than a precise imitation here.

Cast well ahead of the predator, and pull the fly *away* from it. No bait in its right mind will run toward an enemy, and trout are particularly put off by a fly being stripped toward it. Often trout and bass will strafe the shallows and retreat to the safety of the deep to gulp down their prey and then return for repeated helpings. In this scenario, put the fly into the bay and simply wait for the trout to return rather than risk casting over the working fish.

When pursued, Group II fish invariably run *with* the current. Rather than cast down and across the river like most streamer anglers do, match the actions of the prey and cast upstream so your retrieve follows the current. Often, simply hanging the pattern in the river and allowing the current to flutter the marabou or rabbit strip is a lifelike enough presentation to entice fish that might be put off by a retrieved imitation. Nothing beats a Woolly Bugger or Goblin for a hanging presentation.

Group III. Bottom-dwelling fish. Our classic example is the sculpin. Sculpins hug the bottom and move with short hops or bursts barely above the streambed. Rather than speed, these guys rely on their cryptic coloration to avoid predation. The

sculpin

camouflage must work well enough, but on the Truckee at least, the bellies of large browns contain an inordinate number of sculpins.

Sculpins are my go-to pattern when fishing "big" and crayfish patterns aren't working. After much trial and error, I'm convinced that a Woolly Bugger with a heavily hackled head is as effective as the more intricate and realistic ties. Not only do they fish as well, but I don't mind losing these simple flies to the river.

A natural sculpin presentation must keep the fly close to the bottom. Since I am hard-pressed to sit on the bank with a Woolly Bugger anchored to the streambed like the natural sculpins, I dead drift the pattern like a nymph. Most of the weight is in the form of split shot a few inches upleader of the fly rather than built into the pattern itself. The split shot ahead of the streamer forces the fly to dance as it chases the weight on a slack line.

Group IV. Fish eggs and sac fry. It is safe to say that most baitfish get consumed before they learn to swim. An egg drifting in front of a trout has a life span equal to that of a sandwich left on the floor in front of a black Lab. Just about everyone has dead drifted egg patterns, but relatively few have used the equally effective imitations of a sac fry.

Sac fry are translucent wisps of fish that carry bulging yellowish orange packets of nutrient in their abdomens. After they hatch from the egg but are not yet strong enough to swim, these sac fry wallow in the gravel and digest themselves. One to two months after trout or salmon have spawned, the riverbed will be littered with these helpless yet nutritious morsels. Try high-sticking a sac fry imitation just for grins; you will be amazed at its killing effectiveness.

Bait isn't just for the beach chair and Bud crowd. Use your head, read the water, and consciously figure out which baitfish group applies to your conditions. Employ the same deductive reasoning to justify your bait selection and presentation as you would a dry fly or emerger.

Now for the final exam: What baitfish group does a tarpon fall into?

14

Blackflies Are Hell

Bornean ground hornets have driven me to my knees. I've had bloodsucking mosquitoes fill my body with dengue fever. I've had snail larvae eat through my skin and nest in my liver. I've pulled blood-engorged leeches from my crotch and Lyme-infested ticks from my armpits. I've been lashed by jellyfish, slashed by piranhas, bitten by rattlesnakes, and pecked by a duck. I've been a meal to many.

From personal experience and from the bottom of my heart, I can solemnly swear that nothing is worse than the blackfly. Blackflies are the spawn of Satan, the Son of Sam, and the sum of all unfulfilled carnal desires rolled into one. Blackflies are hell.

Blackflies in Africa and Latin America drink the tears of small children and infect them with the blinding nematode *Onchocerca volvulus*. In some West African villages, 30 percent of the inhabitants have been blinded by the blackfly. Canada plays host to severe outbreaks of blackflies, and their attacks have had devastating effects on the cattle industry. Caribou, maddened by swarms of the nasty biting insects, have stampeded over cliffs in attempting to escape.

Lisa and I backpacked across the desert near Palm Springs, where we met the White River, fat and seething with spring melt. After days in the desert, the water was a glorious treat, but it came at a price—blackflies. These weren't the blinding blackflies of Africa nor were they the savage biting bastards of the tun-

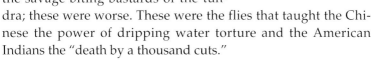

adult blackfly

dra; these were worse. These were the flies that taught the Chinese the power of dripping water torture and the American Indians the "death by a thousand cuts."

The blackflies of the White River never land. They simply buzz millimeters from your eyes, and ears, and mouth, and nose. The only time they actually touch is when they get trapped between your eyelashes during a blink, or inhaled by a breath, or pushed into your eardrum by a loud noise. A loud noise such as the ranting of your blackfly-plagued partner.

I lay on the banks of the White River contemplating the wonderful relief of drowning myself to escape the menace, but as I lowered my face to the water and released my final breath, I saw silver bubbles corkscrewing skyward. When the bubbles hit the water's surface and popped, out sprang blackflies. There was no escape—the river itself was seething with the vermin. All I could do was hobble along the river's edge, up into the San Bernardino Mountains, yelping and madly slapping my face. I went insane that day and never fully recovered.

Blackflies have been around for 180 million years. My theory is that they drove the dinosaurs extinct. Their scientific name, *Simulium*, means something like "snub-nosed being." The name is apt in that most blackflies are easily identified by their squat bodies and pug faces. There are more than fifteen hundred species, whose habits vary wildly, but they all share a single trait:

Their larvae live in water. When trout share the same water, and they often do, blackflies can be very important fare.

The life of a blackfly starts when the female alights on the shore or a midstream rock. She deposits her eggs in the mud or right at the waterline where lapping wavelets can draw the eggs into deeper water and unleash the devils within. The baby flies drift with the flow until they find some suitable object upon which to infest. It might be a stick or a rock or even the back of some hapless crayfish.

The blackfly larva spins a silken pad from which it hangs by a hook-shaped proleg. As an additional anchor, it fixes itself to the pad by a strand of silk. The wormlike larva sports several fans, which billow in the current to sieve fine organic particulate matter from the drift. The larva will sway to and fro to catch errant bits of flotsam or even lower itself into richer food lanes by rappelling down its silk belay line. If food becomes scarce or the environment hostile, the larva can move along the substrate by scrunching itself along on a second proleg (actually a false proleg known as a pseudopod).

Larvae often live in dense colonies of thousands or even hundreds of thousands. Any angler who has turned over but a few rocks in the riffles has undoubtedly encountered mats of blackfly larvae affixed to the stones. The faces of waterfalls are often blanketed with their colonies.

Blackfly larvae are good. They filter out debris and cleanse the environment. They are food to many benthic organisms, including stoneflies, caddisflies, and trout. But just as kittens grow into cats, blackfly larvae grow into winged sadists.

The larva evolves into a pupa that looks a lot like Jeff Goldblum in the classic movie remake of *The Fly*, with wing pads hunched over the shoulders like some wizened troll, and huge round disks covering the nascent eyes hidden beneath. Dreadlocks of gill filaments dangle wildly in the flow. It is awful.

If you were to pick up a rock covered with blackfly pupae, it would feel as if it were smothered in a blanket of hard Rice

The blackfly pupa has characteristic spiracles that dangle above its head like Medusa's snakes. This evil impression only hints at the true horror the adult fly can inflict.

Krispies. The calcified sheath in which the pupa evolves provides strong protection against almost any aquatic predator. When the adult is ready to emerge, the puparium fills with gas, and then its lid pops open. The bubble rises to the surface with the fly hitching a ride inside. As soon as the bubble breaks the surface film, the fly zips into the air in search of trouble.

Blackflies are small, but like the midges they are often confused with, they hatch in such numbers that trout often key in on the ascending adults. The imitation is simple: I dub a ball of black Antron on an appropriate-size hook (18-22) and then treat it with a dry-fly desiccant such as Frog's Fanny or Shimazaki's Shake. A small split shot is sufficient to carry the fly to the bottom, and as the line tightens, the bubble-encrusted black fluff swims to the surface like the real deal.

If you're lucky, you'll catch a trout, but if you're real lucky, the blackflies in your neighborhood will be too busy causing misery elsewhere to ruin your day.

15

Blood Midges

The dead zone. So utterly dead that corpses barely rot. They linger in the dark and the cold, soft lumps of meat delicately smothered by an ever-thickening blanket of silt and slime.

The zone can be black or brown or gray; it is never green. What sunlight might penetrate here has been sucked dry of its life-giving energy, and plants don't survive. Without plants, the process of photosynthesis can't charge the environment with oxygen, and without oxygen, the zone is dead.

Limnologists identify the dead zone as the hypolimnion. The waters of the hypolimnion are so dense that the currents of the warmer, lighter, oxygen-rich environment overhead don't mix. On the lake's surface it can be Victory at Sea, but in the dead zone not a wisp of silt will reflect that turbulence. When plants and animals die, their bodies drift through the warm, biologically active zone (the epilimnion), break through that abrupt shift in temperature known as the thermocline, and continue their downward plunge into the cold, dark, and still.

The dead zone is a niche harboring a limitless source of nutrients and is devoid of predators. Any organism that could exploit the zone would thrive in extraordinary abundance. And one creature does just that.

The Chironomidae is one of several families of midges. Members of this diverse family are better known to the angler as Chironomids. Among the Chironomids is a subfamily called Chironominae; these guys are the blood midges.

Chironominae larvae are brilliantly red and if inadvertently squeezed will burst like a pricked blood blister. This "blood" is red because it is loaded with hemoglobin, the same stuff that makes our blood red. Hemoglobin has a profound affinity for oxygen, and the tremendous density of hemoglobin in this midge's blood allows it to thrive in environments nearly devoid of oxygen—environments like the dead zone.

The blood midge larva burrows into the muck, where it undulates for minutes on end. This writhing motion stirs the water around, and whatever tiny amount of oxygen might be available becomes fixed to the hemoglobin. When the insect hemoglobin (more correctly termed 2 heme, high affinity hemoglobin) becomes saturated with oxygen, the midge larva rests to feed on the nutrient-rich slop in which it resides. At this point the larva can survive in a completely oxygen-free environment. When the oxygen stores are depleted and the larva enters into anaerobic metabolism, the midge once again commences its oxygen-scavenging dance.

Limitless food and no enemies. These guys have it made in the shade. The only downfall might be a lack of privacy. The living is so cushy that thousands, no, *tens* of thousands of midge larvae live shoulder to shoulder. Densities of fifty thousand larvae per square meter are not uncommon. This is a good thing if you're a fly fisherman.

Blood midges abound in all mud-bottomed lakes but are most prolific in the alkaline lakes of the western United States and British Columbia. In lakes that have an abundance of bait-

Most midges make up for their small size by hatching in smothering numbers, as seen here near Klamath Lake. The blood midge, a relative giant compared with its brothers, provides the best of both worlds—it's a mouthful and hatches by the thousands.

fish, blood midges are frequently *the* most important dry fly on the water. Many lakes, such as Martis, historically had huge *Callibaetis* hatches, but the introduction of voracious trash fish quickly thinned the mayfly populations. The blood midges continue to thrive unmolested in the dead zone.

After a few weeks or months (there is huge discrepancy among members of this group, and environmental factors such as temperature and water chemistry influence growth) of groveling in the slop, the larva enters a period of pupation. The pupa matures quickly, frees itself from the mud, and swims in a squirming fashion toward the surface. The puparium is filled with gases that give the pupa buoyancy and help its ascension. For the first time in its life, the midge enters the world of predators.

The gas-filled translucent pupal sheaths backlit by the relatively bright sky turns the pupae into shimmering orange sparks. The effect is extraordinary. Standard pupal imitations look like someone's idea of a bad joke. A Brassie gives off a coppery shine that appears lifeless next to the real deal; however, as traditional imitations go, it's much better than most.

I personally like a thinly dubbed body of bright orange Antron ribbed with copper wire for weight. I treat this with powdered floatant to encase the bug in a flashy, transparent bubble. The pattern doesn't look good enough to sell to humans, so I don't try. I tie it for myself and sell it to my finny consumers. They pay with tugs.

The ascending pupae finally bump up against the underside of the lake's surface film. This film is like a rubbery skin, and the job of the pupa at this point is to punch a hole through this skin to create an escape hatch for the adult midge. I've watched pupae bounce repeatedly off the tough skin until their heads finally break through.

blood midge

Then the pupal skin (exuvia) splits at the shoulders and the adult midge slowly squirts out. As the adult emerges, the tube-like exuvia reveals itself to be almost colorless, very similar to the plastic wrapper that protects a drinking straw. Invariably there are a few tiny bubbles in the sheath, and they, along with the transparent membrane itself, sparkle conspicuously.

Only after most of the adult has wriggled out do the legs pull free and settle down on the water. The whole effect is very smooth, delicate, and efficient. Compare this with a mayfly, which emerges by dragging itself out of the opaque and messy nymphal exoskeleton by clawing with its feet against the surface tension. From a trout's vantage, a mayfly emerger and a midge emerger are as different as night and day.

The emerger is the life stage most vulnerable to predation. The larvae, of course, are immune to predation because they live where fish can't. The ascending pupae are eagerly eaten;

however, since these guys are scattered throughout the water column, it is relatively inefficient for trout to graze on them. At the surface, all pupae stall out in a single strata, and it is here that trout congregate to feed.

Some trout key in on the preemergent pupae, and a few seem attracted to the recently freed winged adults. Most fish, however, want the emergers, and few trout would ever pass one by.

Martis Lake, a profoundly rich blood midge (and trout) habitat near my home, became the laboratory for my efforts to create the better blood midge emerger. The result was the Martis Midge. It kicks butt, if I do say so myself.

Tie on a couple strands of pearl Flashabou so they dangle beyond the bend of a size 14 or 16 dry-fly hook. You only want to create the illusion of the transparent, sparkly, trailing exuvia; anything more is counterproductive. About the worst possible material for a midge shuck is the opaque marabou found on so many patterns.

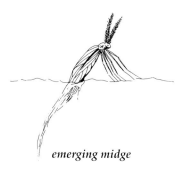

emerging midge

Make a thin, nontapered body of Umpqua's "crayfish" Antron dubbing two-thirds of the way up the shank. Tie in a slender post of bright orange elk so that it doesn't flare and so that it extends over the eye of the hook at a forty-five-degree angle. Finally, make two or three wraps of furnace hackle at the base of the post in the traditional, nonparachute style.

emerging midge fly

Treat the fly and leader with floatant, and then heave it and leave it. If fish are rising to midges around yours but won't grab it, trim (gnaw) the elk hair down to just a nubbin. At times they selectively want the pre-emerger and that's what you just made.

The blood midge seems to stir the proprietary nature in people; everyone wants to claim it for himself. I've heard it called the Crane Prairie midge, the Crowley midge, the Hebgen midge, the Tunkwa midge, and even the Martis midge. By any name, it's a bloody good insect.

16
Blue-Winged Olives

"Blue-winged olive" doesn't refer to a particular mayfly, but to any of several *Baetis* mayflies of the Baetidae family. These members of the Baetidae should have been called Borntodie, because they are best known for hatching in suicidal conditions. Wind, waves, and cold weather are universally recognized as impediments to a successful hatch and, as such, are shunned by your more normal mayfly species. Blue-winged olives are not normal.

The blue-winged olive (BWO) can, of course, make a credible showing on bright, cheery days when birds sing and bees buzz, but their importance to anglers reaches full crowning glory when ducks fly backward, exhaled breath clatters to the ground, and hands are too cold to put in your pants much less in the water to release a wet and slimy fish. The BWO creates one of the most dependably miserable hatches known to man or beast.

Baetis nymphs are quick swimmers that dart to and fro among the cobbles and weeds. They seem to be attracted to drooping grasses and sedges that sweep the river from atop

undercut banks. BWOs are frequently the most abundant mayfly
in many trout streams. Not only
are they numerous, but they have
the ability to multibrood
and in perfect situations
may cycle through
three hatches per
year.

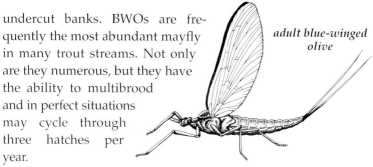

adult blue-winged olive

BWOs tend to be small, size 18 to 24, which can be kind of a
drag when you're trying to thread the eye or see your bug on the
water. Next time you curse their inconvenient size, however,
remember that it is this diminutive stature that frequently makes
the *Baetis* hatch more important than sheer body count. Though
they're zippy swimmers, they simply don't have the power or
mass to break through the film at will. During cold conditions
when the meniscus is at its toughest, *Baetis* nymphs will repeatedly bounce off the rubbery film as they attempt to emerge. It is
not uncommon for a nymph to drift a hundred feet or more
immediately under the surface. The film is a killing ground.

Even when wings are on the water and the eyeballs of rolling
trout are clearly visible, it is a good idea to try a nymph or
emerger pattern in, or just under, the film rather than a high-rid-
ing dun. Often it is very difficult to pick out the low-floating bug
amid the masses, and a BB-size wad of indicator putty pinched
about 6 inches from the bug will greatly assist in making the grab
visible.

Once the duns leave the water, they fly to streamside vegetation to chill for half a day or so, and then they shed their
exoskeletons to expose the sexually mature spinners. The male
spinners leave the bushes and form bobbing clouds above the
water. The females fly horizontally through the eagerly bouncing
horde of males, find a mate, and quickly cop a wad of sperm.

The *Baetis* spinner fall normally occurs about twelve hours
after the hatch and frequently coincides with the next emergence

pulse. I enjoy walking through fly shops and looking at all the beautiful *Baetis* spinner patterns with wings spread and bodies ribbed. Only in the delusional mind of the artful fly tier do BWOs drop lightly to the water like fallen angels. In the real world, they actually crawl underwater and lay their eggs on submerged rocks, logs, and the riverbed itself. As they descend into the wet, a shimmering bubble is captured between the wings, and the mayflies breathe from this reservoir like a Jules Verne bottom walker.

It is interesting that a significant component of the "ovipositing" mayflies are actually males. Once mating takes place, the survival of the males has no genetic significance; those that lived long enough to pass their DNA can die in the bushes or join the females underwater—nature doesn't care. All animals are born with both male and female chromosomes, and it is common for each to carry some of the other's traits if it isn't a genetic liability.

The Baetis *does not lay eggs on the water like a normal mayfly, but instead crawls underwater to affix eggs directly on the streambed. The insect has no gills and breathes directly from the bubble trapped between its wings. A significant number of males (like the one seen here) accompany the females in the underwater journey.*

That male *Baetis* follow an urge to lay eggs is no more ridiculous than the nipples on my hairy chest. From a fish's perspective, both the male and female *Baetis* look like animated diamonds wandering about the submarine realm.

Baetis spinners are very buoyant and seem to have a difficult time retaining a grip on the streambed. They very deliberately lift and place one foot down at a time; sometimes they will reach out with a foot and tap the substrate in front of them as if they are testing for the best foothold. When they get lost to the current, it is all over; the mayflies don't struggle, swim, or attempt in any way to save themselves. They passively float to their doom.

Baetis spinners are unique in that they "fall up," floating upward wings-first. When they hit the surface film, they immediately get flipped and adhere to the meniscus on their sides. The wings remain stuck together holding that bubble of air, and from underwater it looks like they have a single wing sprouting out the top of the thorax. The spinners that reach the surface get stuck *under* the film, making them nearly invisible to the angler looking down into the water. Clots of *Baetis* spinners float up and collect beneath rock ledges, undercut banks, and any other overhead trap. Trout will take *Baetis* spinners in current seams and other "typical" feeding lies; however, most fish graze along the riverbed or move to the *Baetis* traps during heavy ovipositing.

When imitating *Baetis* spinners, I tie a Pheasant Tail Nymph, but before pulling the wing case forward, I tie in a tuft of white poly and split the wing case around it and bring it together at the eye. The entire fly gets thoroughly treated with powdered floatant.

I chew on a split shot about 4 inches up the leader from the fly, which gives me good control of the presentation while allowing the buoyant fly to shuck and jive with the currents like a natural. I'll swing the fly into undercuts or the underside of any structure that might act as a trap to the upward-floating naturals. Foam lines and scum pockets are obvious collectors of buoyant *Baetis*. Once the feeding lies have been cherry picked, fish the fly with a high-stick technique or a Leisenring lift. By bouncing it near the bottom and then allowing it to swing to the surface, you are doing a very credible job of imitating the hapless spinners that have lost their footing and are falling skyward. Like I said, blue-winged olives aren't normal.

17
Brachycentrus

If Martha Stewart were an insect, she'd be a *Brachycentrus*. Their little homes are perfect. Most caddis grab a stick here or pebble there, glue together something that sort of resembles a tube, and call it home. The *Brachycentrus* (brack-ee-SENT-rus) will have none of that. They find the perfect piece of material and chew it down to the perfect size. In some creeks, pine needles are the building material of choice; in others, it might be lodgepole bark; and in still other waters, it might be strips of sedge. Regardless of what the material is, the *Brachycentrus* builds a perfect home.

Their cases are shaped like chimneys that are slightly narrower at the base than at the mouth. The corners are mated to create impeccable right angles, and the square profile is clean and neat. With all the power tools in the world, I certainly couldn't make any-

Brachycentrus *larva in case*

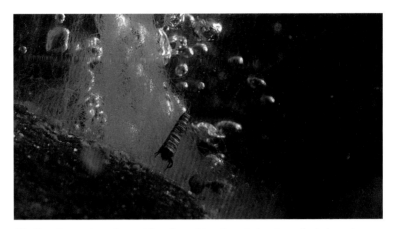

The Brachycentrus, _housed in a log cabin–shaped structure, feeds by out-stretching its "arms" and capturing passing bits of detritus._

thing so flawless, so how can a damn insect do it with only its teeth?

Brachycentrus inhabit a wide variety of habitats but seem to prefer rollicking waters punctuated with numerous back eddies and calm pools. Many authorities refer to them as strictly lotic, or river dwellers, but I have found them clambering along wave-swept shorelines of high mountain ponds.

Brachycentrus are not limited to moving on their own six feet. In our aquariums, I've watched them over and over again crawl up on the fizzing air stone to grab a bubble and hitch a ride on the ascending globe of air. When the bubble hits the surface, the larva envelops the bubble with its legs and somehow prevents it from breaking through the film and bursting. They will ride these bubbles for hours at a time.

I thought this was amusing but aberrant behavior caused by their unnatural environment, until I saw the exact same thing on Rush Creek near Mammoth Lakes, California. The _Brachycentrus_ were harvesting oxygen bubbles being released by aquatic vege-tation as by-products of photosynthesis. They would pluck the bubbles and ride them to the surface, where they would drift round and round a slow eddy. This bubble-harvesting technique must aid their dispersal drift. Most aquatic insects drift downstream at periodic intervals. Called *behavioral drift*, this practice spreads their numbers throughout a river system and ensures that their species won't be annihilated should some catastrophic event affect a section of the system.

Brachycentrus gather much of their food by holding their legs outspread and filtering bits of debris from the current. These larvae are often found in tremendous numbers wafting amid clumps of filamentous algae with their second and third legs spread wide. They are also commonly found atop rocks, each with one lip of its house glued to the rock.

Thread spinning is well known among *Brachycentrus*. These threads are reportedly used as anchors while the caddis rappel downstream, but I feel they use the threads more to lower themselves into prime food-collecting currents. On an eastern Sierra stream near June Lake, I have observed several thousand *Brachycentrus* feeding while dangling by their silken threads. They would rappel into the confluence of two currents and, while being buffeted about, spread their second and third legs wide to gather drifting particles. After some amount of time, ranging from minutes to hours, these larvae would jug back up the threads to the point of attachment. I never once saw them rappel to a downstream perch.

The threads are strikingly visible, and trout will swim through the tangle of threads with mouths wide open like baleen whales to inhale the hapless nymphs. The shiny thread is enough of a trigger that the savvy angler will brighten the tippet with a white grease pen (Mean Streak brand) or typewriter correction tape when fishing a *Brachycentrus* imitation.

As far as imitating the larvae in its log cabin case, I've never seen any specific imitation, nor is one needed. A Pheasant Tail Nymph seems to work just fine. With its concentrically wrapped body that mildly flares to an abdomen with a few scraggly legs, it is close enough. Lighten a foot or so of tippet with a Mean Streak grease pen, and then add a hefty split shot just above the light-ened section.

Flip the fly across and upstream, and allow the shot to hit bottom so the nymph dangles downstream on the taut white line. This technique apparently was developed in the northeastern United States after the turn of the century, and then perfected on the Truckee River in Nevada and California in the early 1940s. When the technique was first developed, white sewing thread was used instead of marked-up monofilament.

When the time comes to pupate, the *Brachycentrus* larva glues the lip of its case to a rock and seals up the mouth of the case with a silk door that quickly hardens. Safely snug inside, the larva transforms into a pupa that matures over a period of one to two months. Upon emergence, usually in spring or very early summer, the pupa chews through the door and swims and crawls along the riverbed.

Unlike many caddis pupa, the *Brachycentrus* pupa doesn't seem to be a particularly strong and active swimmer. It allows the current to push it around and only occasionally attempts to reach some sort of destination. After an undetermined amount of time, the pupa rises to the surface and drifts under the film. Although it is frequently reported that *Brachycentrus* emerge from their cases and then "shoot" to the surface, my observations indicate that they can spend *hours* exploring the riverbed before ascending.

The *Brachycentrus* hatch can be incredible. This is the bug responsible for the famed Mother's Day caddis hatch on the Yellowstone. This is the first super hatch of the year, and anglers from around the country descend on Livingston praying that spring melt won't blow out the fishing.

In May 1998, record snowpack was turning into record runoff and fishing was terrible. On a hunch, Lisa and I went to a small spring-fed creek on the off chance it might not be blown out. We call this Caddis Creek, the maps call it something else, and you can call it anything you like should you stumble across its waters . . . just don't write about it. From a hundred yards away atop a hill in the meadow, we looked down on the creek and could see working trout. Lots of them.

This creek creates wide blankets of foam in the oxbows and back eddies. The rising trout punched black holes in the foam as they rose to *Brachycentrus* emergers and ovipositors. The water was boiling with fish. *Brachycentrus* pupal husks formed ankle-deep clots along the shoreline, and windrows of drowned and drowning adults wafted in trailing streamers along the eddy seams. Beat-up winged adults returning from their egg-laying chores skittered across the surface toward shore. There wasn't a footprint in the sand.

As is common with heavy *Brachycentrus* hatches, individual trout were keying in on specific phases of the "hatch." Some fish were gently tipping up with open mouths breaking the surface, then tilting back down. These fish were taking dead ovipositing adults as well as crippled and dying emergers. Size 14 E/C Caddis and chocolate and green soft-hackles were taken without hesitation as long as the drifts were absolutely drag-free.

Other trout were porpoising through the film. This rise is often characteristic of fish taking emergers just under the surface. Indeed, the soft-hackles and Crippled Caddis patterns failed miserably on these fish, but a green and brown LaFontaine Sparkle Caddis drifted under a greased leader connected with regularity.

Still other trout were not really rising, but golden flashes underwater indicated that they were grabbing either ovipositing adults or ascending pupae. Because both the pupae and swimming adults were carrying packets of air and actively moving about, a size 14 Bird's Nest rubbed in powdered dry-fly floatant, weighted with a split shot, and given an active retrieve would have taken these fish. To be honest, we didn't try. Who wants to nymph while fish are eating drys?

These guys missed Mother's Day by a few weeks, but who cares? It couldn't have been more perfect.

18

Butterflies
The World's Biggest Hatch

Imagine a hatch of four-inch insects that lasts for two months. Pretend that this hatch didn't come off for just an hour or so after sunset, but lasted from dawn until dusk and the numbers of insects were measured in the millions. Imagine the trout that would come to the surface to gorge on the bounty. People would travel the world to fish such an event, and their fly boxes would be stuffed with a myriad of adroitly tied imitations.

In the spring of 2001, such a hatch descended upon the Sierra, and maybe six people fished it. Though that year's event was of Woodstock proportions, it happens to some degree every spring and early summer. It is not really a hatch but an invasion—the invasion of the killer butterflies.

That year's invasion occurred in two massive waves. The first assault started just before opening day of trout season. Blizzards of bright orange painted ladies (*Vanessa cardui*) swept across the Sierra, and thousands found themselves dashed into trout-filled waters. This invasion was caused by a wet year in the deserts of northern Mexico and the U.S. Southwest. The resulting vegetation (and one of the best desert blooms in recent memory) created a nearly limitless food supply for the ravenous *Vanessa* caterpillars.

The caterpillars pupated and hatched into what entomologist Mark Honeywell of Arizona precisely counted as "millions upon untold millions" of winged adults. Like tourists fleeing suburbia on the third of July, the butterflies poured northward in search of refuge from the masses. And just like the fleeing tourists, they succeeded only in bringing the masses with them.

The main avenue of escape was the Great Basin corridor between the Rocky and Sierra Mountains. The butterflies winged their way as far north as British Columbia and Alberta, Canada. Along the way, they colonized likely looking places in which to start families.

Painted ladies are highly adaptable insects and are among the most common of all butterflies; in fact, they are sometimes referred to as cosmopolitans. As our painted ladies were exploding northward out of the arid deserts of America, painted ladies (probably Muslims) were migrating out of East Africa and invading Israel. Painted lady websites litter the United Kingdom, and butterfly-watchers worldwide predict and monitor the migrations.

Several weeks after the first invasion of butterflies hit the Sierra from the south, a second assault appeared from the west. Nurtured by a mild winter in the Coastal Range and the Sierra foothills, California tortoiseshell butterflies (*Nymphalis californica*) migrated into their summer breeding range of the lodgepole and ponderosa pine belt of the upper Sierra. Entomologists on Yuba Pass documented more than a hundred thousand tortoiseshells streaming over in a single day. The most famous wintering grounds for the California tortoiseshell are the slopes of Mount Shasta. Every five to ten years, massive populations of these bugs explode and *millions* of butterflies will fly outward from the mountain. Tortoiseshells from Shasta have been found as far

Tortoiseshell butterfly caterpillars can populate an area
with such dense numbers as
to completely strip the vegetation of its leaves. The
resulting hatch and migration create one of the world's
most underappreciated
hatches.

away as Mexico and British Columbia. Car wrecks have been
attributed to butterfly-slickened roadways.

At the start of any year, it is difficult to predict how successful the caterpillar hatch will be. A hard freeze or a few feet of
snow might kill off most of them. If the winter is benign, gos-
samer webs will likely bloom into silken tents covering most of
the *ceanothus* and bitterbrush of the Sierra. Inside the tents,
squadrons of squirmy brown caterpillars will be doing their best
to devour the landscape. One can wander amid the spice-scented
fields of *ceanothus* and listen to the crunch of a million tiny caterpillar jaws.

On the eastern Sierra, where the dominant vegetation is
inedible sage, the loss of the highly nutritious bitterbrush leaves
can make the difference between life and death to mule deer during a long, cold winter. The bitterbrush fields are so critical to
mule deer survival that wildland firefighters have let man-made

artifacts burn as they devote thin resources to protecting the brush. (Bitterbrush thrives in areas of frequent and light fire. Unfortunately, fire-suppression practices have led to the development of unnaturally dense fuels that burn hot enough to kill the roots of the plant. Stands of bitterbrush burned more than a decade ago have yet to regenerate.) For some species, "the attack of the killer butterflies" is more than a just a whimsical story title.

As is always the case, one species' loss is another's gain. Birds and trout are the hands-down winner when butterflies litter the landscape.

In the spring invasion of 2001, the trout didn't notice the subtle difference between the two species of butterflies, and apparently the anglers didn't notice the butterflies at all. The trout gorged on the lepidopterans while most anglers continued to drift Beadhead Prince Nymphs. Lake Tahoe isn't famous for its dry-fly fishing, but a few fishers in the know were slapping Sofa Pillows and Stimulators into the rocky shorelines and being rewarded with pissed-off rainbows in excess of two feet long. A friend of mine did autopsies of several gorgeous blue-backed Tahoe rainbows and found their stomachs were gorged with the butterflies.

California tortoiseshell butterfly

The butterfly "hatch" isn't as predictable as, say, the pale morning dun or the green drake hatch, but neither is it so unpredictable as to be shrugged off as an anomaly. Every spring will bring with it a butterfly hatch of some degree of magnitude. Leave a space in your fly box for a few Sofa Pillows just in case you encounter a blitz. The truly possessed might even invent a pattern to match such a hatch.

19

Callibaetis Mayflies

Few insects are more important to the stillwater angler than the *Callibaetis*.

In some lakes, damselflies provide explosive angling for unusually large trout, and on other waters, fish wouldn't survive but for the presence of midges. But taken as a whole, no bug dominates more stillwaters than the *Callibaetis* mayfly.

Callibaetis (pronounced cal-uh-BAIT-is) are highly tolerant of ecological extremes and will be found in alkaline desert ponds, roadside ditches, sewage treatment plants, and even tidal marshes. It seems, however, that the *Callibaetis* is best suited for those waters that nurture trout, and every weedy lake that holds trout *will* have its population of *Callibaetis*.

The *Callibaetis* nymph is available 365 days of the year, and it predictably hatches throughout the entire fishing season. The *Callibaetis* is a fly fisher's dream—it acts in predictable ways, and trout key in on that predictability. The angler who takes the time to understand the ways of the *Callibaetis* will cross rods with far more trout than he imagined possible.

The *Callibaetis* belongs to the Baetidae family of mayflies. The Baetidae are extremely important to the fly fisher because many of its members are multibrooded—that is, the nymphs mature exceedingly fast, and several generations will emerge within a single season. Compare this to the average mayfly, which hatches only once in a brief annual flurry.

The *Callibaetis* is the most perfectly proportioned of all the mayfly nymphs. The head is slightly narrower than the shoulders, and the slender body tapers to three equal-length tails that are about as long as the body. Seven pairs of heart-shaped gills fringe each flank of the abdomen. The sweeping antennae are more than twice as long as the head is wide.

The coloration of the *Callibaetis* is as variable as the waters in which it dwells, and the nymphs can change color quickly to match their environment. Because of the tremendous variation in the color of *Callibaetis* nymphs, most trout are not too picky when it comes to the coloration of the artificial. The earth-tone hues of the Pheasant Tail Nymph seem to be universally accepted by even the most finicky fish.

The nymphs have neither skin nor bones; they have instead a semirigid exoskeleton that must be periodically molted. The typical *Callibaetis* might undergo twenty or more such molts throughout the winter.

Early in spring, gases begin filling the void between the exoskeleton and the body within. As the pressure builds, the exoskeleton starts to swell and the nymph becomes unnaturally buoyant. The exoskeleton stretches thin and radiates a shimmering glow as light reflects from the taut skin and interior gases. Perhaps to lessen the uncomfortable pressure, the nymph starts crawling upward. This isn't happening to a lone individual, but to dozens, hundreds, or perhaps thousands of nymphs at the same time. Up the reeds, up the rocks, up the stumps, and even up the legs of wading anglers, these nymphs migrate toward the sun.

When these swelling nymphs lose their footing or try to swim, the buoyancy in the trapped gases lifts them away from

The Callibaetis *nymph looks dark brown out of water, but when viewed from below the surface, the gas-extended exoskeleton of the preemerger glows yellow and gold.*

familiar surroundings and they desperately swim back down to the protective cover. Soon they will lose footing again and once more be buoyed toward the surface, and once again the nymphs will struggle back down to cover. To the scuba diver, this looks like a beautiful dance as showers of glistening nymphs bob up and down over the weed beds. To the trout, it looks like breakfast.

Every morning, all season long, this dance is taking place. The trout grow attuned to the daily rhythm and come to expect the meal that is rightfully theirs. The knowing angler will oblige them.

Get out on the water around 9 A.M. There may be a few spinners from yesterday, but unless trout are working the surface, ignore them. Rig up a floating line with a standard nine-foot leader, and then guesstimate the depth of the water you are about to fish. To the end of the leader, tie on a 6X tippet one and a half times the depth of the water. In eight feet of water, you'll use a twelve-foot tippet. Tie on a Pheasant Tail Nymph of the appropriate size (we'll get to that in a second). With a series of roll casts, work out the line, leader, and that hellacious tippet. You will be pleasantly surprised that the tippet isn't as ghastly as you might have imagined. Lay the line out over the water and be happy as the tippet piles into a big heap.

The nymph will immediately begin to sink, pulling the skinny tippet down with it. Start counting, "one one-thousand, two one-thousand, three one-thousand," and so on. As the tippet dives through the film, it will create a V-shaped wake, with the point of the V facing the angler. When the V turns into a circle or dimple, it means the nymph has landed in the weeds and is no longer pulling the leader downward. At this point, stop counting and remember the number. For the sake of this example, let's pretend that number was eight.

Retrieve the nymph and pull all the weeds off the hook. Cast out again, watch that V, and start counting. At seven, draw in line with the stripping hand, and make one very slow, very long strip until the stripping arm and hand are extended behind you. Trap the line against the cork with rod hand and let the nymph fall. Watch that V!

By retrieving at seven, you stopped the nymph just short of the weeds. The long, slow strip does a good job of imitating the nymph being buoyed to the surface, and the subsequent fall of your pheasant tail mimics the real nymph's frantic return to cover. This is what the trout expect. When the fish inhales the pheasant tail, the nymph will, of course, stop sinking, and the leader will no longer be making a V. It will come to a standstill, and the water's surface will simply dimple around the leader. If the fish starts to swim with the nymph (usually they never stop swimming; they just intercept the nymph and keep on cruising), the V will reappear, pointing in the direction of the trout's travel. Tighten up.

The 6X tippet might seem like a terribly fine connection between you and those lake hogs, but not to worry! Because the tippet is so long, it harbors tremendous stretch and will easily control most trout. The skinny tippet is necessary to cut through the water with a minimum of resistance as the nymph falls.

As the morning progresses and the gases continue to build within their exoskeletons, the nymphs acquiesce to nature's

The sexually immature Callibaetis *dun has characteristic light-colored veins on a dark wing background.*

demands and rise to the surface to hatch. At the surface, they hold just beneath the film with only the hump of the thorax breaking the meniscus. Within moments, the thorax splits and the adult emerges. The mayfly pulls its head and then its legs out of the husk of the exoskeleton. It sprawls the legs out across the water and, levering down against the surface tension, draws the wings and abdomen out of the shuck. Only the tail remains in the husk, and then it too pulls free, leaving the mayfly to drift across the surface of the lake as it hardens its wings.

In the spring, the insect is dark, sooty gray so that it will quickly absorb the sun's warmth. As the hatches progress through the season, the *Callibaetis* are born with increasingly lighter hues to reflect the hot summer sun. In the fall, as temperatures drop, the mayflies once again emerge in the darker colors. The bellies of *Callibaetis* are always lighter than the dorsa. No matter the season, all the *Callibaetis* have distinctively light-colored veins that contrast with the relatively dark wings, giving them a speckled effect, hence the common name speckled dun.

As the majority of the nymphs drift up from the bottom and converge on the surface, so do the trout. Here the feeding is easy and at times gluttonous. The fish often disregard the nymphs and duns to feast on the hapless emergers. The emergers can neither swim nor fly away, and the trout feed at their leisure.

I use two patterns to imitate the emergers: the Quigley Cripple, originated by Bob Quigley, and the Bivisible Dun. The Quigley Cripple hangs at an eighty-degree angle in the water so that the marabou on the distal end of the shank dangles in the water like the discarded exoskeleton. A few turns of hackle hold it in the film, and a post of elk hair creates the silhouette of the upright wings of the emerging dun. It is a classic killing pattern, but the Bivisible Dun is even more so.

The shuck of most stillwater mayflies does not dangle *below* the emerging dun but is stuck against the tacky underside of the film and extends *out* from the emerger. On a Bivisible Dun, the translucent Z-Lon hangs just below the film and looks amazingly like the slipped shuck of the real bug.

The Bivisible Dun is a sparkle dun pattern with an upright post of white calf body hair stacked against a post of black calf body hair. The beauty of the bivisible post is that the fly can bob into and out of shadows or glare, and one or the other post colors will be easily seen. I use this pattern for fishing just about any mayfly hatch when visibility is compromised. When hatches are dense, the bivisible post acts as an exclamation point, telling the angler exactly which fly is his. Even on heavily fished waters with discriminating trout, such as the Henry's Fork and Silver Creek, the fish don't seem to mind the odd-looking wings. The Bivisible Dun also makes a great midge pattern because it can be seen even when fished on size 24 and 26 hooks.

A nice thing about fishing emergers is that size isn't too important. The nymph might be a size 12 and the dun a size 14 (remember, the dun had to fit inside that nymph), but the emerger can be fished all the way to a size 10 because it is imitating a part of the nymph as well as part of the dun.

Once the duns leave the water, they'll retire in the lakeside vegetation to hide from the desiccating rays of the sun. The

The spread wings of the hatching Callibaetis *spinner display their characteristic trace of speckles along their leading edges.*

following morning, the duns will begin walking around in circles and shudder and shake and act like they ate something awful. The wings spread and quiver, and then magically the thorax bulges open and a new mayfly quickly and efficiently emerges from the body of its old self. This new incarnation has translucent wings with only a trace of splotching on the leading edge. Like the dun, it has hind wings that are useless, shriveled stubs. The forelegs are spindly, the eyes unnaturally large, the twin tails beautifully long and graceful. This is the sexually mature spinner.

The spinner has no mouthparts, and the digestive organs have been replaced by reproductive ones. These are winged sex machines that have but one goal in their short-lived existence. About midmorning (or sometimes in the evening), droves of males rise from the riparian growth and form clouds of insects that fly high into the air and flutter back toward earth. When they reach the level of the riparian canopy (often nothing more than clumps of sagebrush), they burst heavenward once again and repeat their fall.

During the fall, the males are releasing pheromones that waft downwind and attract the goggle-eyed females. Thus aroused, the females flutter into the bobbing frenzy of males. From your float tube, it is easy to discern the males acting like crazed yo-yos while the females execute crisp horizontal patterns through the melee. The insects briefly copulate in flight, and then the males go off to die.

Just about the time the morning hatch is winding to a close, the female spinners arrive to lay their eggs. These are the mayflies you most often find crawling all over your body and car during lunch. The female *Callibaetis* whisk along the surface of the water and dap their abdomens into the film to release showers of fertile eggs. The eggs hatch almost immediately and the cycle begins anew.

adult
Callibaetis

Callibaetis spinners can cause tremendous frustration. You may have fished great during emergence, but suddenly you find the fish no longer want your fly. The trout are still rising, but the pattern that was so successful twenty minutes earlier is being ignored. Anticipate the spinner fall. The burnt-out females (spent spinners) have no strength left after laying their eggs and wind up on the water with wings flush against the surface. To you, they can be tough to see, but to trout they are very visible indeed.

As soon as spinners start landing on your arm or the trout begin to refuse your fly, tie on a spinner imitation, but not just any spinner. Most spinner patterns are junk.

The wings of the spinner had to fit inside the exoskeleton of the dun. To fit, they were folded up nice and neat like geisha fans. When the wings unfolded, they didn't unfold all the way, but retained their pleats. When the crystal-clear, corrugated wings of the spinner lie flush on the surface, water is drawn into the folds, which bend rays of light every which way. Tiny bubbles trapped under the pleats sparkle like silver pearls.

From an underwater vantage below and a few degrees to the side of the spinner, the wings are like windows. Through them the sky, the clouds, and the seagulls are clearly seen. This is in sharp contrast to the water on which the spinner is bound, which is reflecting the dark bottom of the lake. From directly beneath the spinner, those pleated wings now glitter like diamonds and spew rainbows like the microprisms that they are. Compare that to the artificial burnt chicken wing pattern that looked so cool in the fly shop.

The best spinner patterns are barely there: a little fuzz on the hook and a wispy loop of Z-Lon to suggest the possibility of wings. A couple strands of sparkle organza add flash and a prism. Not perfect, but usually good enough. The CDC Biot Spinner also works well, because it too has sparkle organza and the fluted CDC feathers trap air like the real spinner wings.

The multibrooded *Callibaetis* emerges in the spring as a size 12. About six weeks later, the progeny from the first hatch will emerge, but they will be a size 14. Six weeks later, the next brood will hatch and be a size 16, and so on until the end of the season, when *Callibaetis* in October are popping off in a minute size 20. Every six weeks or so will be a major emergence period, but enough bugs are out of sync that *Callibaetis* hatches can be counted on virtually every day of the season. The nymphs of the season's last brood, having all winter to grow, will emerge the following spring in a succulent size 12 to start the cycle once again. I'll be there to meet them.

20

Clinger Mayflies

Next fishing trip, indulge your wild side and spend time snorkeling in white water. It's cheap, easy, and probably no more dangerous than base jumping at night or driving while reading the newspaper.

Grab a mask and snorkel, and then find a stretch of calm, friendly river just downstream of a rockin' bit of white water. Start at the bottom of the rapids and claw your way upstream in about two feet of water. You want to be deep enough to experience the river but shallow enough to breathe from your snorkel while clinging to the streambed.

On a serious note: There are severe life-threatening safety hazards associated with swimming or wading in moving water. Never, ever attempt this unless you are under the direct supervision of an experienced practitioner. Really.

There are many advantages to clawing upstream rather than gliding with the current. First of all, it's great exercise and will keep you warm in the chilly water. Second, your silt plume will be trailing rather than enveloping you. Third, you retain absolute control over your progress; drifting with the current too often speeds you past cool stuff, and sometimes the hydraulics will playfully stuff you under a logjam or into an undercut bank. Fourth, and most important of all, clawing upcurrent allows you to become one with the mayfly nymphs.

Stop trying to survive long enough to wrap your arms around a boulder and rest. Take a couple of slow, deep breaths through the snorkel (clear as much water as possible first) and relax. Enjoy the surge of the current as it massages your shoulders, listen to the clack of cobbles being bounced toward the ocean, and watch as the water slides above you like quicksilver taffy. Within a few seconds, the terror will subside, and you'll be overcome by a sense of peace and tranquility as you realize what an alien, yet truly perfect, world you have entered. The bliss might also be due to an endorphin rush or advanced hypothermia.

Now, look at that boulder you're clinging to. Rest your nose on it so your field of vision is skimming right over the top of the rock. You will notice that the boulder is coated with zillions of threadlike green stalks that wave and waft gracefully in the current. It will undoubtedly remind you of an aquatic chia pet. These green hairs are filamentous algae (one of the periphyton, organisms that live attached to underwater surfaces), which form the foundation of the aquatic food chain. Look closer at these periphyton, and you'll notice something truly remarkable: Only the tips of the algae actually are moving with the current. In a world where your every effort is dedicated to hanging on to that rock, these tiny weeds are as unruffled as if they were relaxing in a hot tub.

In even the most tumultuous waters, there is a zone right along the streambed called the boundary layer, where currents cease to exist. The friction exerted by the rocks, sticks, and old truck tires protruding from the river's floor slows the water to a virtual stop. The water in this zone diffuses with the moving water above it rather than mixing through turbulence. Compared with life in the main flow, existence in the boundary layer is a walk in the park.

A cadre of mayfly nymphs have chosen to take up residence in this park. These nymphs are flattened to best take advantage of the thin calm zone. Some are hydrodynamically shaped so that the current above them actually helps press them against their bouldery domain.

The legs of these nymphs are broad and strong, splaying out to the sides for maximal gripping force. The gills are adapted to press against the rock, and in some nymphs these gills can even cup to create suction against the substrate. (Some entomologists aren't quite convinced this is so, but I'll toss my hat in with the group that believes it.)

All of these nymphs have eyes on top of their heads rather than to the front like most. The bulging eyes create a distinctly fat face profile, and any nymph you might encounter whose head is wider than the rest of the body belongs to the family of mayflies known as *clingers*. Even as

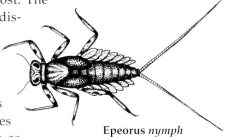

Epeorus *nymph*

duns and spinners, the clingers retain the distinctive shovel-faced profile. In the lexicon of aquatic entomologists, all clingers are members of the Heptageniidae family.

A few years ago the western Heptageniidae family was split into eight genera. Most of these splits were based on minute differences in the nymphs and are of little importance to the angler and even less to the trout. In the interest of simplicity, I'm going to pretend the splits did not take place and will discuss what used to be the four important genera of the region: the *Epeorus, Cinygmula, Rhithrogena*, and *Heptagenia*.

It is easy to tell the Heptageniidae nymphs apart. Remember, all Heptageniidae have heads that are wider than the rest of the

The Epeorus *is one of the most important of the clinger mayflies. Here an* Epeorus *dun prepares to molt into the sexually mature spinner.*

body. If the nymph has two tails, it is an *Epeorus*. Just that alone should get rid of half your collection. Everything else will have three tails.

Look down on the bug, and if it has little points jutting out from its cheeks, it's a *Cinygmula* (or the smaller, much rarer *Cinygma*, but just pretend it's a *Cinygmula*).

If the nymph has three tails and no pointy cheeks, flip it on its back; it won't like this, but ignore its feeble protest. If the gills do not overlap, it is likely a *Heptagenia*; if they do overlap, it is probably a *Rhithrogena*. (Note the disclaimers "probably" and "likely"; there are exceptions, but for our purposes, these rules are good enough.)

Of all the Heptageniidae, the *Epeorus* is far and away the most important member for western anglers. In Sierra waters, *Epeorus* outnumber all other Heptageniidae combined. *Epeorus* (and the new genus *Ironodes*, which was split from the *Epeorus*) nymphs live in the fastest sections of river. Because *Epeorus*

The exoskeleton of the dun splits at the thorax, and propelled by gases, the fully formed spinner is slowly expelled from its former self.

nymphs are such tenacious clingers and don't drift, I rather doubt they are very common trout fare; however, so many famous anglers have made such a to-do describing *Epeorus* nymphal imitations that I won't go so far as to categorically state they are unimportant.

I *will* state that *Epeorus emergers* are hugely important to trout and largely misunderstood by trout anglers. Unlike most mayflies, which emerge on top of the water after the nymph has ascended to the surface, the *Epeorus* dun crawls out of its nymphal exoskeleton while the nymph is still clinging to a riverbed boulder. In some instances, the act of emergence will loosen the nymph's grip on the riverbed, and emergence takes place within the water column.

The freshly emerged dun carries a pocket of carbon dioxide within its crumpled wings, and the buoyant gas helps the dun ascend through the water column. Once on the surface, the dun's wings dry and harden, and the insect flies away. From an under-

Note the glassy wings, huge eyes, and long forelegs and tails of the sexually mature spinner. All digestive parts have evolved into sex organs, and the spinner has only a day or two to mate and lay eggs before it burns up its energy stores.

water vantage, the ascending *Epeorus* dun looks like nothing more than a dark blob tangled in dangling legs and shimmering wings. A soft-hackled fly with a peacock herl body and a partridge wing is an excellent imitation, especially if it is treated with a dry powder floatant to help it retain a shiny pocket of air.

High-stick this pattern with a split shot heavy enough to sink the air-laden fly to the riverbed. At the end of the drift, allow the line to tighten, and swing the fly toward the surface like a naturally ascending emerger.

The *Rhithrogena*, commonly known as a March brown, inhabits the same turbulent habitat as the *Epeorus* and shares the underwater emerging trait. That same partridge and peacock soft-hackle works equally well for both bugs. Like the *Epeorus*, the *Rhithrogena* will often spend long minutes drifting about the surface while its wings dry, and the dun imitation can be important.

As the name suggests, March browns are typically found emerging in the spring. About the time the *Rithrogena* are finished emerging in early June, the *Epeorus* launch into action, and you can expect to find them appearing throughout the summer months.

I like a low-silhouette parachute dun pattern with the hackle wrapped around a post of white calf tail stacked against a post of black calf tail. This bivisible wing stands out well against the alternating dark and flashy turbulent waters from which the *Rhithrogena* emerges.

Cinygmula and *Heptagenia* (as well as *Nixe* and *Leucrocuta*, which used to be *Heptagenias* but were recently given genus status of their own) emerge in the more traditional fashion. These clingers dwell in quieter reaches of freestone streams, where their nymphs swim to the surface and emergence commences in the film. A Humpy makes an excellent emerger imitation, because its buoyant deer-hair shell floats it well in the bouncy water, and the moose-hair tail penetrates the water to somewhat resemble a slipping exoskeleton.

Next time you visit clinger country, be sure to carry a pocket full of soft-hackles, Bivisible Duns, and Humpies. And don't forget your mask and snorkel.

21

Corydalus

Hellgrammites

The name *Corydalus* dances brightly off the tongue and brings a light and airy image to the mind. It could be a delicate plant bearing sweet-scented, dainty blossoms that sway with the breeze. It might perhaps be a small bird that sings sweetly from a twig and brings a smile to all those who hear its voice. You might even name your firstborn daughter *Corydalus*.

Imagine your newborn baby girl swaddled in warm, fuzzy pink hospital blankets. The nurse hands you the tiny bundle, and you gently pull back the blanket to reveal the first glimpse of your precious baby. With a shriek, you attempt to dash Cory against the tiled floor, but she is far too fast. With a lightning-quick thrust, she snaps jagged mandibles into your face and drives them deep with a deliberate chewing motion. As you learn too late, *Corydalus* is not a little bird or a dainty blossom; she is a hellgrammite.

They say that beauty runs skin-deep, but hellgrammites are butt ugly from the very first molecule of their sallow epidermis.

They are nothing less than four fleshy inches of unfettered ugliness. The thorax is adorned by the usual half dozen legs, but the segmented abdomen sports an additional eight pairs of rubbery gills that wriggle like dark, pointy nipples . . . witch's nipples. At the end of the abdomen is a pair of grappling hooklike appendages. By comparison, a stonefly nymph looks like Gwyneth Paltrow.

A baby hellgrammite is something only its mother could love . . . to eat. The most thought-provoking appendages of the hellgrammite are its gnashing jaws, and even Junior is fair game if he gets in Mama's way. *Corydalus* seeks her prey among the cobbles and leaf packets of freestone trout streams and rivers. Like Gollum, she despises light and forages in the darkest reaches, only truly exposing herself at

hellgrammite larva

night. She tracks by sight and scent, and nothing is safe from her jaws. The rubbery body is admirably adapted to squeezing itself into the narrowest confines. Prey that finds cover among the few interstices too narrow to accept *Corydalus* must still dodge the probing mandibles she sweeps to and fro in the cracks to dislodge the hapless animals cowering within.

The same mandibles that are the thing of macroinvertebrate nightmares are also admirably suited to defending *Corydalus* from her predators. Kids know hellgrammites as "toe biters," and any angler who has carelessly attempted to catch hellgrammites can attest to their bellicose nature. A "baby" one-inch larva can easily draw blood from a callused thumb. Rumor has it that ingested hellgrammites have been known to kill trout by chewing through the fish's stomach.

Despite their powerful jaws, nasty disposition, and ugly looks, *Corydalus* is a featured item on the menu of many a

Hellgrammites flow over the streambed like living smoke. Their flattened, rubberlike bodies allow them to pursue prey into the smallest interstices.

carnivore. Trout, crayfish, egrets, and of course, other *Corydalus* eat hellgrammites like many-nippled chicken sticks. Hellgrammites spend two to five years as larvae, and their importance as trout fare is not dictated so much by their numbers as by their longevity. Hellgrammites can swim but prefer to crawl across the streambed. When hunting, they stop and start while continually swinging their heads back and forth as they probe the nooks and crannies for prey. When being pursued, they literally flow across the substrate like a ghastly magic carpet.

It is probable that trout meet hellgrammites only by happenstance, and it is highly unlikely that they would key in on any specific hellgrammite trait. A pale, earth-tone (gray, tan, light brown) strip hair leech or soft-hackled Woolly Worm pulled close to the riverbed would be as good as any other approach to "matching the hatch."

The actual hellgrammite hatch occurs in the dirt and is of little importance to trout or pursuers of trout. The larvae crawl from their watery home and roam the countryside until they find suitable substrate in which to pupate. This search can carry them a hundred yards or more from water. Once suitable ground is found, they build a pupal chamber in which they reside for a few weeks or even months before commencing actual pupation. Unlike a soft and cuddly moth pupae (cocoon) or a gorgeous butterfly pupae (chrysalid), the pupal *Corydalus* sports toothy jaws and eagerly defends itself from would-be aggravators.

About two weeks after pupation begins, the adult *Corydalus*, now better known as a dobsonfly, emerges from the dirt. With crispy, translucent wings held tentlike above her body, the female looks like a cross between a caddisfly and a stonefly. Like her former incarnations, she can bite like the mother she is soon to be.

The male dobsonfly looks like a lab experiment gone amok. Imagine some crazed genetic engineer crossing a woolly mammoth with a stonefly and you'll get the general idea. Like the female, the male has translucent, tent-shaped wings, but he also sports wicked crossed mandibles that are more than half as long as his body. In the de-mented fashion of everything *Corydalus*, these

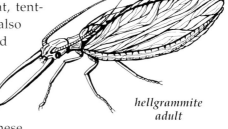

hellgrammite adult

tusks are sex toys. The bigger the better. During copulation, the male grasps the female between his sicklelike jaws and holds her just tight enough that she can't run away while he impregnates her. No doubt he gives her the occasional love nip just for the spice of it.

Terrestrial dobsonflies are just as nocturnal as their aquatic counterparts and are rarely seen by anglers. They spend the daylight hours hidden under leaves and in dark crevices. Dobsonflies live for about a week, and it is unlikely that they feed. The females lay chalky egg clusters on leaves and twigs that overhang water. When the eggs hatch, tiny *Corydalus* drop into the water and the terror begins.

22

Craneflies

More than six hundred kinds of craneflies live in North America. They range from three-millimeter tiny dancers to the massive leatherbacks that sprawl a full four inches across my office wall. The fourth edition of *American Heritage Dictionary* defines ecotype as "the smallest taxonomic subdivision of an ecospecies, consisting of populations adapted to a particular set of environmental conditions. The populations are infertile with other ecotypes of the same ecospecies." Craneflies provide perfect examples of ecotypes living shoulder to wing pad: Some larvae live in loose oak litter, some dwell along sandy shorelines, others reside under submerged boulders, and others yet prefer aquatic moss beds. They are all the same, only different.

The cranefly larva is commonly encountered in tailwater fisheries. The cranefly most frequently associated with our trout streams is the small yellow *Tipula angustipennis*. The larva dwells in riverine moss and woody debris. It has extremely weak prolegs and is easily dislodged when water levels fluctuate. It is a small (three-quarter-inch) grubby-looking thing that could easily be mistaken for a legless, decapitated caddisfly larva. The missing head is practically diagnostic for the cranefly larva. The head is there, of course, but it is retracted into the body and invisible to the casual observer. A soft squeeze will pop it out like a sclerotic zit.

The little yellow craneflies emerge in early spring and are usually abundant by opening day of trout season. Congregations of the craneflies accumulate on spray-drenched faces of freestone boulders. I don't have any idea if they are mating, ovipositing, or just hanging out and shooting the breeze, but frequently there will be a dozen or more huddled close together. Next to the wings of a cranefly are clearly visible club-shaped projections called halteres. Halteres supposedly aid in navigation and help maintain equilibrium during flight. God obviously needs to work on these things because craneflies are reckless fliers and even worse landers. I've watched over and over again as a cranefly crash-lands into a congregation of cohorts and sends them scattering . . . sometimes into a trout-filled river.

I have frequently observed craneflies vibrating. Like skinny bobbleheads on caffeine overload, these bugs quiver and lilt from side to side in a frenetic effort to accomplish something. But what? Internet searches and repeated calls to University of California Davis and University of California Santa Barbara have not brought me closer to answering the question. Are they communicating, releasing pheromones, or perhaps keeping rhythm with a celestial jukebox? I'd like to know.

Craneflies are often mistaken for daddy longlegs. Daddy longlegs, or more correctly, harvestmen (phalangids), have long gangly legs but are completely unrelated to craneflies. Harvestmen are eight-legged arachnids, not insects. Interestingly, I've watched entire colonies of harvestmen blanket the walls and ceilings of caves, where they quiver and vibrate like the cranefly.

Harvestmen are well known for being the most highly venomous spider in the world; if its fangs were long enough to penetrate human skin, it is said, a single bite could kill several grown

The cranefly is nothing more than a gigantic midge. It has a face like a moose, legs like a movie star, and a larva that trout go bananas over.

men. Sounds great except that harvestmen a) are not spiders and b) don't have any venom whatsoever. Urban legends die hard.

Unlike caddisfly larvae, cranefly larvae apparently don't practice behavioral drift and as a result are unlikely routine items on the trout menu. When stream levels fluctuate during hydro releases, summer rain events, or recreational pulse flows, cranefly larvae become waterborne in catastrophic drift. The larva can swim with a leechlike undulating motion but more commonly curls into a protective ball that tumbles along the bottom until it encounters friendly water. After summer thunderstorms, my go-to pattern will be a contrasty streamer, a San Juan Worm, or a larval imitation. The larval cranefly imitation consists simply of gray buggy dubbing covering the hook shank. The commercial versions include a dark "head," but now that you know the cranefly larva doesn't have a visible head, you can guess what I think of those flies.

Cranefly adults oviposit by laying eggs on the damp, wave-lapped shoreline or by skimming the surface and dragging the tip of the abdomen across the film. This skimming behavior can

drive fish nuts. Early one May I spent an
evening on the Lower Yuba and was
utterly confounded by the
exploding fish that stead-
fastly refused my
flies. You could
see the wakes
in the water as
they surged for-

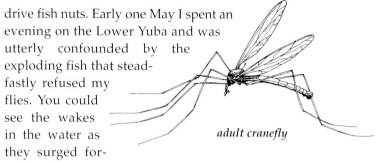

adult cranefly

ward then lunged through the film. It was not until I turned the
light on in the truck and a huge cranefly bounced inside the
windshield that I got a clue.

It is the ovipositing cranefly for which the famous skating
spiders were developed. Spiders are nothing more than very
long, very stiff hackles wound on the hook. Tied right, they balance on the water by the very tips of the hackles. The flies can be
swum across the water by tossing a mend downcurrent of the fly
and allowing the tension to drag the pattern. The better way is to
use a very long (sixteen to twenty feet) and light leader during
breezy conditions. Hold the rod high in the air, and have the
wind capture the leader and skate your offering across-stream.
Try to keep all the line off the water so that your skating spider
looks like tumbling thistledown. Never put grease on these patterns; dress them only with desiccant powder so they stay as
light and buoyant as possible. The chases are amazing and the
grabs downright illegal.

23

Crayfish

If Darwin had stumbled across crayfish rather than finches, the theory of natural selection would have been put on hold for a millennium. These crustaceans are slow, dumb, easy to see, and taste good. Their favorite diurnal habitat is in dark, tangled places—the same places preferred by hungry brown trout.

In the Truckee, the river with which I'm most familiar, crayfish are the food of choice for brown trout over fifteen inches. Why in the world would a large trout swim to the surface to suck in a small insect when, with less effort and less exposure to predators, it could eat an eight-ounce crayfish?

Crayfish is a seasonal dish. During the winter, crayfish hide under rocks or dig into the streambed to escape the effects of flood and ice. High spring flows will uncover a large segment of the crayfish population and mercilessly grind them to a pulp under churning rocks and boulders. Drought years are even more lethal. Trapped in the shallows, crayfish get frozen in place or macerated under drifting anchor ice.

A single crayfish has the nutritional value of hundreds of insects. In crayfish-rich waters, it is invariably the food of choice among bigger fish.

The relatively few crayfish that survive to spring find a smorgasbord of relatives upon which to dine. Crayfish grow quickly in the nutrient-rich and warming waters. Unlike humans and fish, which have internal bone structures called endoskeletons, crayfish have their "bones" on the outside. These exoskeletons don't grow and must be periodically shed.

The crayfish shell requires a tremendous amount of calcium to develop—more calcium, in fact, than a nutrient-poor Sierra water can normally supply. As molting grows nigh, the crayfish absorbs the calcium from its shell and stores it in a pair of white disks in its thorax. These white disks are called gastroliths, literally "belly stones." Mergansers and mink enjoy frequent crayfish meals, and the midstream boulders or bankside landing pads upon which they dine are frequently littered with discarded gastroliths. The resting lies of large trout, especially brown trout, can sometimes be identified by the litter of gastroliths that pass through the fish's guts undigested.

Crayfish retreat to some dark cranny to molt and hide until their fresh shells reabsorb the calcium and harden. The "soft-

Trout go crazy for crayfish. These wild, normally reticent rainbows overcome their normal shyness to brazenly pull chunks of crayfish from my hand.

shell" state can last up to a week, and trout and bass are suckers for tender crayfish.

I have not found any studies that scientifically investigate the trout-crayfish relationship, but several are available on smallmouth bass-crayfish. Smallmouths, even very large ones of four and five pounds, have a decided preference for crayfish one and a half to two and a half inches long. When given a choice, they took postmolt softshell crayfish over hardened ones. On nothing other than a wild leap of faith, I'll suggest that trout possibly have similar dietary preferences. I'm sure this hunch will get repeated a few times and become fact. Such are fishermen.

There are 366 species of crayfish in North America. Trout and smallmouths will eat them all. Though crayfish vary in size and armament, they all tend to match the color of their habitat. They come in various shades of gray, brown, orange, green, and even blue. The softshell incarnation of all these crayfish is a very pale version of the hardshell. Knowing that smallmouth bass and *possibly* trout key in on the soft state, tie your flies in the pale hues.

Crayfish walk around the riverbed facing forward; they march with claws leading the way. When leery, crayfish walk backward away from the threat with their claws raised in defense. When danger is imminent, they dart backward with a burst of rapid tail flips, trailing their claws.

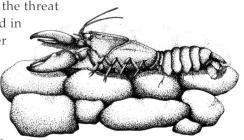

crayfish

The best crayfish presentation is none of the above. The most successful approach is to high-stick an imitation in a drag-free drift like a big nymph. I like to slide the imitation off a set of riffles and then let it fall quickly into the pool immediately downstream. My guess is that this approach imitates an injured or dying crayfish. The take is usually pretty solid, and 0X tippet is fine.

A Woolly Bugger makes a pretty effective crayfish fly. The cylindrical, hackled body with trailing marabou claws is good enough for the fish I hang out with. When given an excuse, even otherwise savvy fish will ravage a crayfish. I will, too, and like an alcoholic with his beer, one is too many and a hundred aren't enough.

A traditional crayfish boil, where you dump a bushel of live crayfish into a kettle of rolling water (no, they don't scream—but Lisa does) seasoned with bay leaves, peppercorns, salt, and lemon peel, is pretty hard to beat. But it can be made even better with Prejean's Crawfish Étoufée from Prejean's Restaurant in Lafayette, Louisiana.

Prejean's Crawfish Étoufée

3 pounds crawfish (crayfish) tails
2 sticks margarine

$^1/_2$ cup flour
1 onion, chopped
2 cloves garlic
2 bunches shallots, chopped (keep tops separate)
1 green pepper, chopped
1 cup celery
3 tablespoons tomato sauce
3 cups water
salt, cayenne, black pepper to taste
1 bunch parsley, chopped
3 cups cooked rice

Melt margarine. Add flour; brown lightly. Add onion, garlic, shallot (bottoms), green pepper, celery, and tomato sauce. Add salt and peppers to taste. Cover and cook about 1 hour. Stir frequently to keep from sticking. Add 3 cups water; simmer for several hours. If mixture is too heavy, add more water. When mixture is creamy, add crawfish tails. Cook 15 minutes or until tails are tender. If mixture thins after cooking, thicken by adding 2 tablespoons cornstarch mixed with water (consistency of cream). Add shallot tops and parsley. Pour over steaming hot rice. Serves 6.

Serve with a tub of Dixie beer on ice. Invite me and I'll bring the pralines.

24

Cut Bugs

When Only Half Is Sometimes More Than a Whole

About fifteen years ago, Lisa came home after a long day of guiding on the Little Truckee. She was bouncing off the walls with excitement. "You have to call in sick and come to the river with me in the morning. The fishing is incredible!"

Always eager to test the mental acuity of my boss, I called the firehouse and said, "You won't believe this, but I'm going to be sick tomorrow."

Suspicions aroused, the chief immediately inquired, "How do you know you are going to be sick?"

"Because I won't be coming to work."

It worked like a charm. He immediately granted me time off and advised me to drink plenty of fluids and get lots of rest.

Taking the chief's words to heart, I had a few extra beers and slept in.

I awoke to a gorgeous June day; the sky was cobalt blue, the air smelled of fresh sage, and the neighborhood was filled with the cheerful sounds of children playing in the street and the screeching of brakes. On the river, blackbirds were calling from the lush bankside willows, and PMDs bubbled up like clockwork. Eyeballs and noses broke the water, and fishing was deceptively easy. Dragonflies began hatching under the warm sun, and soon the sky was filled with the acrobatic insects. It was just another day in paradise.

Then something changed. It was hideous: The fish no longer wanted my flies. The Little Truckee is intimate enough that you can watch individual trout rise to individual bugs. I watched closely for any changes, but they were still visibly gulping PMDs. I tried a different pattern, and then another, and then a finer tippet. The fish continued to feed but ignored my offerings completely. Lisa sat down beside me, made one cast, and hooked a fat rainbow. Then she did it again. With a smug grin, she released her fish and cupped the fly from my prying eyes. "See, I told you the fishing was good!"

For another fifteen minutes, she played coy and continued to catch fish while I watched her every move and couldn't figure out her trick. Finally she swung the rod tip toward me and

showed me her fly. It was a size 16 Quigley Cripple with the marabou "shuck" stripped off. Grinning, she pointed to the dragonflies: "They are eating the mayflies but apparently don't like wings and legs. They're catching the bugs, eating the abdomens, and dropping the thoraxes back to the water."

I scooped up a PMD "emerger," and sure enough, it wasn't an emerger at all, but simply the front half of

dragonfly eating a mayfly

the dun floating on the water. The trout were keyed in to the windfall and eating the cut bugs to the exclusion of everything else. I immediately trimmed down some emerger patterns and started catching fish again. It was a revelation, but at the time I considered it a freak happening.

It may have been a freak happening, but over the past decade and a half, we have repeatedly stumbled across the exact same phenomenon. Several years ago, I spent six weeks kayaking the length of the Sacramento River from the trickling snowmelt above Lake Siskiyou to the San Francisco Bay. Over and over I spent days paddling through swarms of dragonflies and killing fields of mutilated mayflies.

This fall Lisa, Jim Zech, and I elbowed our way into a secret spot on a local river. A good *Baetis* hatch commenced, and fish were rising freely to the bugs. It took about an hour of fruitlessly flogging the water before it became apparent that dragonflies were

Lisa watches a swarm of dragonflies pound a Baetis *hatch on California's Yuba River. Trout become fixated on the cut bugs, and a specific imitation is needed to fool these fish.*

This Isonychia *dun has been high-graded by a dragonfly that wanted only the succulent abdomen.*

once again high-grading their mayfly meals. They were turning blue-winged olives into blue-winged almosts. I tried imitating the cut bugs with spinner patterns, but they failed miserably.

Closer inspection of the cut bugs revealed that their wings were crumpled like half-rolled newspapers. I'm not sure why this was happening, but we saw many dozens of mayflies with their wings held in this distinctive curled position. My guess is that when the dragonflies bit the mayfly bodies in two, the abrupt drop in hydrolymph (bug blood) pressure caused the wing veins to empty, and as a result, the wings lost their structural integrity and imploded. Unlike translucent, flat, sparkly spinner wings, the wings of the cut bugs were narrow and opaque. Once again a trimmed Quigley Cripple was close enough to fool some of the fish but was still far from perfect.

That evening I tied some dedicated cut-bug patterns. I used dun-colored spindles of EP fiber for wings and spun a thorax of deer hair over the wing tie-in. The hollow deer hair would add buoyancy, and I left a few of the hairs long to penetrate the water like the legs of the natural. The following day, a north wind blew and all the dragonflies vanished. Story of my life.

A few weeks later found us filming *Isonychia* mayflies hatching on the North Fork of the Yuba above Camptonville. *Isonychia* typically emerge by crawling onto a rock before commencing ecdysis. As we filmed the nymphs crawling up onto the rocks, it dawned on us that an unusual number of *Isonychia* were hatching midstream. A quick underwater visit of these "emergers" showed that once again we were in the company of cut bugs. About fifty yards upstream of us, a swarm of dragonflies was blitzing the mayflies and littering the river with the winged thoraxes. Though we may have been slow on the uptake, the trout certainly weren't, and they were feeding on the disemboweled corpses with greedy abandon.

Armed only with snorkels and video cameras, we watched as the fish ate their fill. I think our cut-bug patterns will work, but since dragonflies are gone for the season, we'll have to wait for next summer to find out. Meanwhile, I urge you to tie up some cut bugs of your own creation and watch for dragonflies. Good luck!

25

Damselflies

Leona Helmsley reportedly wore a damselfly brooch as she was being sentenced for tax evasion. That she wasn't sporting a dung beetle is no surprise. Dung beetle hat pins and potato bug napkin rings are not frequently seen among the gimcracks of the rich and famous, yet damselfly icons abound. Damselflies are lithe, quick, pert, and delightfully colored. Sporting its likeness subliminally imbues the bearer with these traits. Unfortunately for Leona, her judge was not an entomologist.

Though commonly associated with lakes, damselflies live in every conceivable freshwater habitat. On Silver Creek, when anglers are painstakingly matching size 18 pale morning duns, two-inch-long damselfly nymphs are clambering among the reeds, attracting some of the largest fish in the stream. In the freestone waters of foothill streams, damselfly nymphs are one of the more commonly encountered macroinvertebrates, yet no one fishes their imitation. In Lake Davis, arguably one of the West's most famous destinations for fishing damselfly imitations, the

A damselfly in its typical pose, with wings folded atop its back.

vast majority of fly fishers are wasting their time by fishing the wrong imitations in the incorrect way.

Dragonflies are the sole members of the order Odonata. Damselflies are a suborder of the dragonflies and can be distinguished from the dragons by their characteristic "hammerhead" appearance, created by the large compound eyes that protrude from either side of a relatively small face. All but a few hold their wings upright over their backs when at rest. The spreadwings, which hold their wings out to the side in dragonfly fashion, are easily identified as damselflies because the wings taper to a narrow joint at the base. Dragonfly wings, on the other hand, are as broad at the base as they are at the tip.

To escape the notice of predators, damselfly nymphs cling to stems of tules, rushes, and sedges that are the same diameter as their bodies. When danger approaches, they scuttle like woodpeckers to the safe side of the stem, with only their compound eyes protruding from either side of the stalk. As adults, when it is too chilly to fly, they continue this reclusive habit in the riparian willows. In stream habitats, the nymphs frequently bury themselves in sand, leaving only their eyes revealed to scan the surroundings.

These camouflage tactics not only hide the nymph from predation, but also provide the perfect springboard from which to bushwhack a passing bug. The damselfly nymph has a unique double-hinged labium that tucks underneath its head and over its mouthparts. The labium is held in a cocked position until prey passes, when, driven by the hydraulic pressure of hemolymph being forced into the structure, it jabs outward and snares the food item with its hooked teeth. The prey is pulled back into the mouth, where it is then leisurely chewed to death.

Adult damselflies are equally amazing killers. They hunt in three distinctive styles: plucking, ambushing, and hawking. Damsels are adept at plucking bugs off foliage and even snag spiders out of their webs. They will also perch like accipiters, lying in wait for prey to fly by, then launch into a wild pursuit. And every angler has observed damsels zipping to and fro as they search ("hawk") for bugs on the wing. Prey insects apparently have a comfort zone and won't flee unless a damselfly enters that zone. It recently has been discovered that dragonflies (and presumably damsels) have the ability to appear motionless when in fact they are flying rapidly toward a target. It is the same tactic used by fighter pilots when they keep themselves between a specific feature on the horizon line and a target. How Odonates with pin-size brains are able to process such complicated factors as vector and intercept angles is beyond comprehension.

damselfly

If you think their hunting tactics are cool, you should see them have sex. Most matings are catch-as-catch-can affairs that often border on rape, but some species go through prolonged courtship rituals that can last for hours. I performed an environmental assay in a remote Sumatran jungle, and of all the exotic stuff I stumbled across, my most vivid memories are of watching damsels in courtship. Iridescent indigo-colored damsels perched on twigs and fluttered, flapped, and curled their wings like miniature Thai dancers. Mates arrived from the rattan thickets, and they paired up and silently fluttered off down the stream corridor in a dreamlike, narcotic state. It was nothing short of magic.

Mating among Odonates is bizarre. The male grabs the female, usually behind the head, with an appendage on his abdomen, and moves sperm from the tip of his abdomen to a special receptacle (secondary genitalia) near the base of his abdomen. The female then bends her abdomen up to the secondary genitalia to receive the sperm. In the process, sperm from previous matings (damsels are quite promiscuous) is removed and discarded.

Ovipositing is the stage when adult damsels become extremely vulnerable to predation by trout—in fact it is the most vulnerable stage in a damselfly's life, yet not one in a thousand anglers fishes the imitation.

The female damsel inserts her eggs into a slit she has cut

An adult damselfly deep underwater inserting eggs into the stem of a reed. Note the mirrorlike shimmer of the air that sheaths the bug.

into a plant stem. This is usually on a mat of weeds floating on the water's surface, but a large number of damsels oviposit underwater. The female crawls down an emergent rush or sedge until she is anywhere from several inches to several feet underwater. At this point, she slits the stem and inserts her eggs. Lacking gills, she must breathe free air, and her body is cloaked in a shimmering silver sheath of air from which she respires. These two-inch-long glittering forms are visible from a vast distance, and fish come from afar to feed on the helpless insects. The sight is one of nature's truly wild spectacles.

Ovipositing takes place at the same time that damselfly nymphs are migrating to shore to emerge into adults. Entire flotillas of anglers will be fishing the obvious nymphal imitations when the trout are greedily feasting on the egg layers and ignoring the nymphs. If you watch carefully, you'll actually see the reeds parting as large fish squeeze into the vegetation to graze on the silver-sheathed adults.

When the female is done laying her eggs, she lets go of the plant, and the air surrounding her body buoys her to the surface, where she lies trapped *underneath* the film. Beneath the film, she is invisible to all but the most highly observant angler. To a trout, she is a sitting duck. Many of the rises attributed to trout eating nymphs are actually the demise of spent adults hidden under the film.

The eggs in the plant stems hatch, and out squirm perfectly formed miniature damselfly nymphs. Their lobed tails swish to and fro as they drive the baby naiads toward unwary prey. The tails also act as gills, and in oxygen-poor environments, damselfly nymphs can be seen panting in the weeds, wagging their tails like contented dogs. In the fall on many of our waters, these eighth-inch translucent green nymphs join back swimmers as the main forage items for trout. In the winter, as the vegetation dies, the damselfly nymphs become brown or light yellow to match the background coloration of their environs.

In the spring, just as aquatic veggies are sprouting new green growth, the damsel "hatch" begins. Because the environment is loaded with everything from rotted vegetation from the previous winter to vibrant green new growth, the nymphs can sport a bewildering array of colors. In periods of heavy feasting on damsel nymphs, trout can become color-conscious, and the prudent angler will carry a selection of nymphs in shades of brown, gray, and green. My favorite pattern is nothing more than a few fibers of marabou wrapped up a 2XL shank and secured with an overwrap of fine brass wire. When wet, the marabou becomes translucent and wispy and is as good an imitation as many of the fancy patterns with legs, eyes, feelers, and whatnot, if not a better one. You must remember that I'm a very lazy fly tier and will take the shortest distance between my vise and a fish. My good friend Andy Burk would vehemently disagree with my choice of flies, but we both seem to catch about the same number of fish.

Damselfly nymphs may be imitated at the vise, but they are impossible to imitate in the water. The real deal undulates like the spineless belly dancer that she is. The tail moves in one direction, the abdomen in another, and the thorax in yet another. The motion is synchronous and slinky and seductive. It's fascinating to watch but impossible to imitate—so don't try. Swimming a damsel pattern is an exercise in utter futility that will immediately alert the dumbest fish to your evil intent.

Damselfly nymphs frequently hold motionless in the water, with their bodies tilted about thirty degrees toward the surface. A well-greased leader will hold a motionless imitation at about the same angle, and heave-it-and-leave-it tactics will catch you passels more trout than any attempt at a retrieve.

Like a swimming crab when it spies a permit, a swimming damselfly nymph will make a beeline for the bottom when it sees a trout. If you don't believe me, wave your hand above the next damselfly nymph you encounter and be amazed when it dives for the weeds. So if you *must* retrieve the damn bug, try this: Put a small split shot about one foot up the leader from your nymph. Cast the nymph well ahead of a cruising fish, and drag it into a path of intersection. When you think the nymph is visible to the trout, give it slack. The shot will drop to the bottom, and your

A damselfly nymph has crawled out of the water up a stick to molt into the adult stage.

The nymph's exoskeleton has split at the thorax, and the adult begins to bulge out.

nymph will follow just the way the trout expects it to.

The nymphs that make it to shore crawl up some bit of vegetation to emerge into adults. (The lazy ones just molt in the mud.) The nymphal exoskeleton splits at the dorsum of the thorax, and the winged adult slowly emerges. This pale-colored insect takes twenty minutes to an hour to pump its wings full of fluid to gain enough structural integrity to fly. At this soft *teneral* stage, it is highly vulnerable. Any breeze, or even the motion of a restless trout pushing through the reeds, will be enough to make the teneral lose its tenuous grip and fall into the drink. Countless thousands of tenerals become trout chow every day. Meanwhile, the average angler is tossing and stripping damsel nymph imitations.

Vow to be different and vow to succeed. On your very next trip to a damsel-filled lake, carry some braided-leader-butt adult damselfly patterns in blue and pale green. *Do not* buy those things with the massive thorax, six legs, and blinking eyes. Just a fly with a chunk of braided butt section and a few wraps of stiff hackle is perfect. Shake the blue pattern in powdered fly floatant, and fish it among the weeds with a split shot to imitate the ovipositing subsurface adults. Or if it gets breezy, take one of the light green patterns and drift it around the margins of a nearby weed patch. If you get skunked, at least you met your vow to be different.

The legs have finally emerged, and fifteen minutes after it started, emergence is nearly complete.

The adult slowly wriggles up and outward. Note that the legs are still pinned inside the nymphal exoskeleton, and the slightest breeze will knock the hapless insect into the water.

The freshly emerged damselfly pumps fluid into its wings and waits for its body to harden enough to support flight. The insect at this stage is known as a teneral. It will take several hours for the pale green coloration to shift to the brilliant colors of the fully mature adult.

26

Frogs and Fish

Trout love frogs to death; in fact, they love frogs to extinction. Early Sierra travelers described the tremendous number of frogs that blanketed the mountainscape. Living waves of fist-size frogs would bound into the alpine lakes as humans approached. The range literally seethed with the amphibians.

Today mountain yellow-legged frogs (*Rana muscosa*) are so scarce that scientists scour the Sierra in search of them. What was once one of the most common animals in the High Sierra is on the brink of extinction because trout love them so.

The mountain yellow-legged frog is the only frog native to California whose tadpole lives for several years before sprouting legs. (The bullfrog also has an overwintering tadpole, but it was introduced into the state.) In the stark, almost sterile mountain lakes, where summers are short and winters severe, this multi-year growth strategy has proven to be the frog's fortune as well as its fate.

The tadpoles spend the summers in the warm shallows of Sierra lakes and streams feeding on algae. In the cold winter

The mountain yellow-legged frog was once the most numerous vertebrate in the High Sierra. Today it hovers on the brink of extinction.

months, the tadpoles descend into the depths of the lakes or into areas of moving water to avoid being trapped in ice. As soon as the ice melts in the spring, the tadpoles once again move into the shallows to fatten on the bounty of algae.

After two, three, or sometimes even four years, the tadpoles grow and finally morph into mouse-size frogs, which eventually grow into animals the size of rats. The conversion of simple algae into rat-size packets of protein is of incalculable value to the Sierra food web. Millions upon millions of these frogs formed the food base for virtually every carnivore in the high country. Mink, marten, wolverines, and a plethora of other high-order predators likely feasted on the bounty.

Prior to the mid-1800s, the Sierra was virtually devoid of trout. Out of nearly three thousand bodies of water, the only lakes in the entire range with trout were Tahoe, Donner, and Independence, waters all connected by the Truckee River to the vast Lahontan Sea east of the Sierra. Modern man found the Sierra barren of trout and immediately set forth to rectify the problem. Any

The tremendous numbers of mountain yellow-legged frog tadpoles and their ability to transform algae into big chunks of protein suggest that they are of extreme importance to carnivores of the barren high country.

lake that could be reached by mule train or moderate hiking was planted with trout of various species. Since the 1950s, with the aid of aircraft, almost every single body of water has been planted repeatedly and incessantly with trout. There is no pond too small or lake too remote to avoid aerial bombings of fish.

Sierra trout grew quickly and they grew huge; twenty-inch rainbows and goldens were commonly found in many Sierra waters. The same deep lakes that gave winter refuge to the tadpoles also gave winter refuge to the introduced fish. In these waters where fish and frogs cohabited, angling was nothing short of phenomenal.

As early as the 1920s, a disturbing phenomenon was being realized: The frogs were disappearing from the landscape, and in lakes with trout the frogs were gone. In 1924, biologist Joseph Grinnel hiked across the Sierra, documenting the plants and animals he encountered. In his journal he wrote, "The advent of fish sooner or later nearly or quite eliminates the [mountain yellow-legged] frogs."

No one can say for certain why the Sierra is so devoid of high-order predators today. In most High Sierra locales, habitat destruction isn't an issue, and it has been many, many decades since fur trappers vacated the range. It would seem that animals like the wolverine would slowly but surely make a comeback after trapping and hunting were curtailed, but it just hasn't happened.

Could it be that the mountain yellow-legged frog was the linchpin in the Sierra food web that supported the higher animals? Could our lust for good fishing have led to the demise of an entire ecosystem? Is it worth planting Sierra lakes as we have done for more than a hundred years, or is it time we revisited our motives and management style?

The era of huge trout being commonly encountered is gone, because their food is gone. Many Sierra waters now produce trout with short, skinny bodies and grotesquely huge heads—the hallmarks of a starving trout population. Though these lakes can barely support the minuscule population of trout they contain, more likely than not every other year an aircraft will descend upon the lake and unload another burden of trout. The more intelligent solution would be to return these borderline lakes to the frogs.

Fish and Game biologists agree that there is a much better way to manage our waters; yet their bosses, the politicians who run the department, know that it is the hatcheries that fuel their slice of the government pie. To question the use of even a few hatchery fish in the High Sierra is to question the need for our hatchery system as it exists altogether.

In a state that requires an environmental impact report before one can *remove* a single dam on a solitary creek, it seems the same state would require an environmental impact report on an arbitrary practice that impacts thousands of lakes, thousands of miles of waterway, and hundreds of thousands of acres of the wildest country left in this nation.

Though questions abound, one thing we do know for certain is that trout love frogs, and if there is anything they like more than frogs, it is tadpoles. The best tadpole pattern I know is a golden-bodied Woolly Bugger (I use ice chenille) wrapped in black hackle with a black marabou tail. Tossing one of these Buggers into the chill blue waters of a high Sierra lake and slowly wriggling it toward shore is bound to result in a bent rod and a crooked grin. Yours is the one tadpole that bites back.

27
Fur Balls
Of Mice and Fish

Through the veil of an early morning mist, we could vaguely see lemon yellow floats bobbing atop the still, dark waters of Stampede Reservoir. Russ swung the bow of the state's Fish and Game whaler into the rising sun, killed the motor, and we silently glided between the floats and over the gill nets hidden below. I reached into the chill waters, grabbed the top line, and started hauling the slimy, dripping net over the gunwales and into a rusted milk pail.

The two of us peeled fish from the nylon web and dropped them into a bucket to be weighed and measured. With trout, we took one more step: We cut open the stomachs and cataloged their contents.

The carnage seemed wasteful, yet compared with the biomass of the large reservoir, it was an insignificant blip in the fish population. The data compiled from the biannual netting would provide a firsthand look at the health of the fishery and allow management decisions to be based on fact rather than conjecture.

At least half the fish were tui chubs, a native filter-feeding species that anglers find contemptible for their lack of sporting qualities and propensity to overwhelm a sport fishery. Of the remaining fish, perhaps half were redside shiners and the rest introduced kokanee salmon and rainbow and brown trout. (Today a significant portion of the catch might be smallmouth bass, which were illegally planted into the impoundment in the late nineties.)

As I hauled in the dripping net, we spied a fat brown trout rising from the depths. Its kyped jaw was snared in the net, and the pale, stiff body hung away from the mesh like a ghostly flag. Even several feet below the surface, we could see that he was well fed. The belly of the trout bulged so that it looked as if it had swallowed a dumbbell weight. The brown measured twenty-nine inches and weighed a bit over twelve pounds; a nice fish, but not even close to some of the lunkers that fin in these frigid waters. After scraping some scales into an envelope for later analysis, we autopsied the trout to see what it had gorged on.

The belly meat was crimson—no doubt he had been feasting on the abundant kokanee staging for their annual spawning run. The distended stomach glistened like mother of pearl and unfolded easily beneath Russ's sharp blade. Small black specks in green fluid spilled into the bucket: midge pupae, hundreds of them. As the knife slid further, two fist-size fur balls emerged from the glistening stomach: full-grown chipmunks.

Did these chipmunks decide to go for an evening dip, or did they crash into the water when some tree broke? Did the trout perhaps leap into the air and snag the unsuspecting mammals from a branch? We'll never know for certain, but what we do know is that when the opportunity presents itself, trout will eat large balls of fur.

Trout eat mammals far more frequently than we might imagine. While working as a guide in Alaska, I got pretty bored high-sticking glo bugs and tossing streamers for big fish. To combat the drudgery of dredging, I tried my darnedest to put clients into mouse-eating rainbows and silver salmon on the first day of the trip. If they got only one grab on a skittered mouse, the guests were as hooked as their fish and the rest of the week was cake.

In the North American fishing world, there is nothing, absolutely nothing I would rather do than toss mouse patterns to willing trout and salmon. The mouse pattern itself is all but irrelevant. A golf ball-size chunk of untrimmed caribou hair spun on a wide-gap hook is all that is required. You can add tail, ears, and

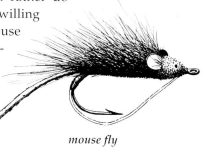

mouse fly

twinkling eyes just to irritate the PETA crowd, but the adornments are unnecessary, add weight, and tend to sink the fly.

The act of mousing is more than visible; it's visceral. First there's the plop of a well-delivered mouse. If the grab is really on and the cast is tight to trout cover, very often the detonation is immediate. Usually, however, you need to swim the mouse in short, erratic strips. Sooner or later a fin-infested mound of water rises behind the mouse, and then the mound swells into a moving wall of water trailing a wake as the fish pumps toward the fleeing rodent.

More frequently than not the trout will miss the mouse on the first grab or two, and with each miss, the fish will return to even more aggressively blow up under the fly. This is the kind of fishing that requires no hook to provide satisfaction.

This kind of fishing exists only in Alaska, right? Hardly. Remember those chipmunks? This may be the Lower Forty-Eight, but the trout at least haven't lost their appetite for really rare red meat.

The first mousing article I ever read was in one of the national bait and bullet magazines. It was about a group of locals who used pipe cleaners to strap hooks to mice, put the adorned mice on shingles, and then floated the rodent-laden craft down-stream. As a shingle approached big brown habitat, the angler tightened on the line and pulled the mouse into the water, with predictable results. The photos that accompanied the article were all the proof I needed that big trout adore fur balls. I must have been ten years old at the time, but the article forever burned the name Alturas, California, in my brain as a very, very cool place to fish.

The first time I actually saw a trout eat a mouse was during an evening PMD hatch at Hat Creek. It was probably a vole that I scared into the water rather than a mouse, but who cares, they look the same. Instead of scurrying back into the tulles like I expected, it lit out directly across a glide covered with dainty mayflies and dimpling trout. It was inevitable that the rodent would get moshed, and we weren't disappointed. About halfway across, the river opened up on command, and the mouse disap-peared into the void. Moses couldn't have done it better.

Lisa and I ran back to the truck for 7-weights and spent the rest of the evening skating big black silhouettes through the drift-ing wings. We experienced some heartrending grabs but never connected. Nevertheless, I'll remember those near misses far longer than any PMD-caught trout that evening.

After one session of mousing Alaskan trout, I returned home to discover that my baggage hadn't arrived with me at the Reno airport—my film was gone. I was under contract for a magazine piece on fur-feeding trout, and the deadline was near. In a des-perate search for photos, I turned to my best friend and partner in crime, Rusty Vorous.

Rusty and I hatched a plan over a large pitcher of margaritas at Hacienda del Lago. It seemed like a good plan. A few pitchers later, as we were being escorted toward the door, it seemed like an incredibly good plan. We decided to get the pictures I needed on the Truckee River, and we knew how to get them. And where.

On a very early morning in September, we met on Fanny Bridge at Lake Tahoe's outlet. I came equipped with the requisite camera gear, and Rusty arrived with a cardboard box filled with dozens of pet-store mice. In the gin-clear water beneath us finned twenty or thirty trout that ranged from one to ten pounds. They looked hungry, so I selected an especially fat mouse from the box and dropped it into the river.

The mouse floated for a second and then started swimming furiously toward land. Tiny pink feet against the thrust of hand-size tails—in the race toward shore, it was no contest. A herd of trout rushed the white fur ball, and when it looked as though one of the leviathans would surely devour the mouse, a small twelve-inch rainbow popped up out of nowhere and snatched the rodent. With barely a hiccup, the mouse was gone. I was absolutely floored. That such a relatively small fish could eat such a comparatively huge meal was a revelation.

By the fifth or sixth mouse, the trout were on to us. As we tossed rodents, the fish would look skyward and, like Willy Mays chasing fly balls into center field, would beeline toward the drop point. The water seethed with enthusiastic trout, and in their rush for breakfast, sometimes two fish would grab the hapless mouse at the same time. At other times a mouse would break free and bob to the surface, where waiting seagulls swooped down and snatched the breathless rodent. The water boiled with trout, and the sky was filled with wheeling, shrieking gulls. It was mayhem of the best kind.

On the fifteenth mouse or so, a funny thing happened. Nothing. The mouse hit the water, swam to shore, and then preened itself as if it had not a care in the world. Rusty tossed in another mouse, and again nothing happened. The only difference was that all the previous mice had been of the white variety; the last two were brown. On a hunch I hucked a chunk of Egg McMuffin, and the trout and gulls were all over it.

These fish are fed a daily diet of marshmallows and bread by tourists on the bridge. In the trout's mind, our mice were moving bread. They had no idea what to do with the brown, naturally appearing, food. My assignment was to write about trout eating mice, not bread, and in those pre-Photoshop days, white mice just weren't going to make the magazine. In a stroke of brilliance, Rusty jumped in his truck and returned from 7-11 with a brown felt-tip pen. We colored the backs of the white mice so they looked kind of like field mice to the camera, but we left their bellies white so they looked kind of like bread to the fish. Perfect.

I put my eye to the camera and told Rusty to let fly with a bivisible mouse. I waited a moment and then told him once again to toss a mouse. When nothing happened, I looked up from the camera and followed Rusty's horror-stricken gaze. It seems JR's restaurant is a popular place for parents to have breakfast with their kids before dropping them off to school. Pressed against the glass were seemingly millions of innocent little faces. Little faces fully absorbed in the spectacle of mice and men. Men who were going to jail.

Rusty shook the box of mice out over the railing. While the river exploded with trout and gulls fighting over the hatch, we scooped our gear and bolted. On the way home, we swung by the Tahoe City post office. In the mail was an issue of *Fly Rod and Reel* magazine with a full-page photo of Rusty captioned, "Guide of the Year." If they only knew.

28

Glossosoma Caddisflies

In nearly every tumbling cold-water stream lives an insect so important to trout that day after day throughout the first half of the season, the fish will often eat nothing else. I consider it to be one of the most important of all caddisflies, yet not one angler in a thousand has ever heard of it. I've never seen an imitation of it in any fly shop, nor have I ever heard of anyone purposely imitating its behavior. I'm willing to bet it is the insect most frequently responsible for anglers snapping their rods in frustration.

What angler hasn't noticed all those little gobs of pebbles glued to instream boulders? Looking for all the world like barnacles left high and dry at low tide, these scabs of pebbles chronicle high-water levels on freestone rivers, creeks, and streams throughout the West. Each and every cluster of pebbles—and in some waters there must be hundreds of millions—used to house an immature *Glossosoma* caddisfly.

The *Glossosoma* is a member of the family Glossosomatidae, the most primitive of all the case making caddis. These guys invented the technique of building a home. Like most inventions, this one was a good idea but lacked some of the more refined qualities of subsequent incarnations. Most caddis larvae make tubular homes, simply extending them as they grow. The *Glossosoma* builds a dome that, like a pair of kid's shoes, must be discarded and replaced as it matures.

At dusk or dawn, huge numbers of *Glossosoma* crawl out of their shelters and release themselves into the current. The numbers are staggering. In one survey, *Glossosoma* larvae attained drift rates of 350 insects per hour through a one-square-foot portion of river. In a stream he was sampling, Gary LaFontaine calculated that a trout with a three-foot feeding area was seeing up to 1,600 drifting larvae in one hour. LaFontaine concluded that during certain times of the year, *Glossosoma* create more selective trout feeding than any other organism. I absolutely agree.

The larva might drift for a few feet or a few hundred yards before it lands on the streambed. It quickly begins gathering gravel and within two hours has built a new home (more properly termed a test). This home is dome-shaped, with a hole on the bottom at each end of the dome. Across the bottom of the dome is a belly band woven from silk.

The pebble case, or test, of the Glossosoma *is igloo-shaped with a silk band across the belly that allows the larva to crawl around like a turtle.*

The larva crawls onto a rock searching for algae and plankton on which to feed. The larva might travel one direction for a while and then turn around inside its case, stick its head out the opposite hole,

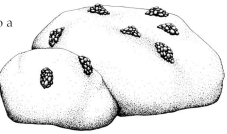

Glossosoma *cases on rocks*

and continue on in another direction. After a week or so, the case again becomes uncomfortably snug, and the larva once more vacates its home and casts its destiny to the current.

Some segment of the *Glossosoma* population is doing this every dawn and dusk throughout the early summer. The heaviest drifts seem to occur about an hour after sunset.

At some point the larva decides it's time to pupate. It aims the holes of its home so the current percolates through, providing a fresh flow of oxygen. Then, for the final time, it glues its case to the rock upon which it sits. This affixing of the larval cases to the cobbles and boulders of the streambed is excellent insurance against getting inadvertently swept into the drift. It also spells certain death should some upstream dam operator decide to abruptly drop the water level. Billions of *Glossosoma* are lost every year as a result of river fluctuations.

After several weeks of pupation, the pupa chews itself free and emerges from the pebbled dome. This sometimes takes place in the morning but more commonly about an hour after sunset. These size 16 burnt orange–colored pupae are very active swimmers. They often congregate in the soft water immediately downstream of riffle areas. The pupae hide among the cobbles during the day, but at dusk they emerge to swim about in an erratic jinking movement.

One or two evenings after the pupa emerges from its rocky home, a pair of sparkling bubbles develop just under the pupal skin at the shoulders. Possibly aided by the buoyancy of these bubbles, the pupa swims to the surface and drifts a short distance (about one minute); then the adult pops out and immediately flies upstream.

About an hour after sunset, adult *Glossosoma* caddis return to the river to lay their eggs. *Glossosoma* are one of the many caddis species that crawl and swim underwater to lay their eggs on the streambed.

Having lost its gills, the adult is an obligatory free air breather and must carry its oxygen supply with it. This it does by cloaking its entire body in a bubble of air. The bubble feeds oxygen to the caddis as it swims and crawls about the streambed. As the oxygen is consumed, the pressure differential shifts and oxygen from the water is drawn into the bubble thus replenishing the caddis's supply.

The bubble-encrusted caddisflies look like nothing less spectacular than sparkling, animated diamonds. In the relative dark of the evening stream bottom, the bubbles reflect the available light and seem to glow from within. To say these guys are highly visible is a gross understatement.

To summarize: Just about every evening of early summer, starting about an hour after sunset, size 16 to 18 pale-colored larvae free themselves from their homes and drift, en masse, downstream. Shortly thereafter, size 16 burnt orange-colored pupae emerge from hiding and start swimming about. Many of these sport sparkling bubbles of air and ascend to the surface and emerge. Only a short time after that, size 18 dark brown adult caddis from an earlier night's hatch return to the river and travel about the streambed to lay their eggs.

The typical fisherman experiences this sequence initially by seeing a sudden burst of caddis adults winging their way upstream. There might be thousands of bugs in the air, on your arms, behind your glasses and in your hair. At the same time, trout are rising, slashing, and flashing at or just below the surface. The excited angler ties on an Elk Hair Caddis and flails the water for about twenty minutes, until the rises stop and the caddis disappear. Rarely does he catch a fish. Frequently he cusses in despair and has been known to stalk off the river leaving a pile of broken fishing tackle in his wake. Sound familiar? You're not alone.

Relax. Get on the water about an hour after sunset. Tie on a size 18 orange-, pink-, or cream-colored larva imitation. Being a hack, I often use a Bird's Nest because it works pretty well and offers the opportunity to immediately switch gears. Add some split shot, and high-stick the imitation downstream in a drag-free drift right along the riverbed. You are imitating the helplessly drifting larvae. Trout are expecting it.

When the first trout rises, or you start to experience a burst of caddis activity, tie on a size 18 Bird's Nest and a small split shot. Rub the Bird's Nest in powdered floatant and lob it out and across the stream. The nymph will be buoyant from the floatant, but the shot will help it break the surface. Actively retrieve the fly with a twitchy and erratic strip. You are imitating the actively swimming pupae. All those rising, slashing fish you've experienced in the past were *not* taking adults—they were chasing down the sparkly pupae just under the surface. That's why they ignored the Elk Hair Caddis.

As soon as the rises stop, and I don't care how many caddis are still buzzing about, reel in that Bird's Nest, make sure it is bone dry, treat it with powdered floatant, and fish it along the bottom of the riverbed with little or no drag. The rises stopped because the trout settled back down to the streambed to graze on the highly visible and vulnerable caddis adults.

If you're in the mood for some dry-fly action (and who isn't), tie on a size 16 Crippled Caddis pattern. With its shuck-trailing, bicolor body, supported by a flared wing and parachute hackle, the E/C (Emergent Crippled) Caddis is a dead ringer for a crippled *Glossosoma*. Caddis are very efficient emergers, but by my own estimation, about 5 percent don't survive the transition, with the adults getting trapped in the pupal shucks.

Five percent of many thousand hatching caddisflies equates to a huge number of bugs that will remain easy pickings for hungry trout. Fish the E/C Caddis immediately following the caddis hatch and use it as a searching pattern throughout the day. Fish are attuned to seeing the cripples and will often suck them in even while other types of insects are available. The E/C Caddis is my default dry fly. If nothing is on the water suggesting I do differently, I fish the E/C. And the *Glossosoma* is one of the reasons why.

29

Go-To Nymph

If I were forced to fish a single fly all season, it would certainly be a size 12 dark gray nymph. Any nymph would work, but since I'm partial to the Bird's Nest, that's the nymph I would use.

The Bird's Nest can be fished any one of a million ways, looks alive underwater, and best of all, is so simple to tie that I don't mind tossing it into snaggy places.

Cal Bird was quite strict with his Bird's Nest recipes and would scold me for using rabbit, mink, or worse yet, synthetic Antron when tying his pattern. Cal insisted the bug be tied with a blend of Australian opossum and coyote dyed with his own secret formulas, which usually consisted of onion skins, coffee grounds, and some sort of explosive such as gunpowder or picric acid. The one aspect we both agreed upon was that a proper Bird's Nest should be tied with wood-duck flank rather than the soft and limp feathers of mallard or teal.

Cal insisted that Bird's Nest be spelled with a lowercase B because, he claimed, the fly was named after getting it tangled in

Bird's Nest nymph

a bird's nest on his home water, the Truckee River. Our mutual friend Polly Rosborough hinted that Cal changed the origin of the name after he chided Cal about naming a fly after himself. Regardless of the origin of the name or whether it's capitalized, it is my go-to nymph.

As I said, a Bird's Nest looks alive underwater, and it never looks so alive as when it is being actively retrieved with short, darting strips. The soft hairs breathe like something possessed underneath the quivering veil of wood duck. These same short, darting strips coincidentally mimic the swimming movement of my favorite real live nymphs—those belonging to the family Siphlonuridae.

The Siphlonuridae include the western gray drake (*Siphlonurus*), the black drake (*Isonychia*), and until recently given a family unto itself, a bug with no common name, the *Ameletus*. Since the *Ameletus* looks and behaves for all intents and purposes like one of the Siphlonuridae, we'll leave them in that family for the sake of simplicity. Trout don't know the difference.

The Siphlonuridae are large mayflies that attract the attention of trout and trout anglers alike. They can be found throughout the country from opening weekend until the last day of the season. The nymphs are various shades of dark gray and average a meaty size 12. Unlike most nymphs, which hide underneath rocks or within the protection of dense weeds, the Siphlonurids

Siphlonurus *nymph*

The Siphlonurus, *or gray drake, typically emerges on emergent vegetation rather than in open water; however, there are so many exceptions to this "rule" that you are wise to carry a handful of emerger patterns when in the vicinity of these gorgeous mayflies.*

brazenly swim about like small fish in open water. They are strong swimmers, but as quick and agile as they might be, Siphlonurids are frequently found on the trout menu.

Siphlonurus gray drakes will be found hatching on ponds and sluggish rivers by April. The nymphs swim to the shallows, where they crawl out onto rocks or up emergent stems to molt into duns. Because of this predominantly terrestrial emergence, many authors insist an emerger pattern isn't indicated. This is unfortunate advice, because more times than not, a segment of the population does not make it to shore to hatch and emerges in open water. Perhaps because they evolved a terrestrial emergence strategy, those that hatch midwater have a higher than normal mortality rate and trout zero in on these emergent cripples. Emerger *Siphlonurus* patterns can be killing.

The standard way to fish the nymph is with that size 12 dark gray nymph affixed to a nine-foot, 4X leader on a floating line. Cast tight to the shore, give the nymph a few seconds to settle in among the scores of naturals, and then strip it back in short darts.

An Isonychia *nymph at rest and another swimming. Notice how the legs are tucked tight, the tail fibers form a single paddle, and the entire body and tail move as one.*

The emerger is even easier: Tie on a large Quigley Cripple or Bivisible Dun, and chuck it somewhere along the shoreline. Don't twitch, strip, or cast repeatedly; a heave-it-and-leave-it approach is the best.

As the season progresses, the *Siphlonurus* hatch will move northward and higher into the mountains. In late June, the hatch will be in full swing at the eight-thousand-foot level of the Kern Plateau and at six-thousand-foot lakes around Truckee.

The kissing cousin to the *Siphlonurus* is the *Ameletus*. Unlike the *Siphlonurus*, the *Ameletus* is a quick-water insect that shares the same habitat as the *Baetis*. Blue-winged olives and *Ameletus* go hand in hand. Like the *Siphlonurus*, the size 12 dark gray nymphs congregate near the shallows and emerge on shore. The hatch is never intense but makes up for lack of density by spanning a solid two months.

In the dog days of summer, the size 12 dark gray nymph will be doing its damage in the highest Sierra and Rocky Mountain

This nymph has locked its tail into a single paddle and is about to burst off the finger and swim to safety. These powerful nymphs can easily cover a foot per second—don't strip your Bird's Nest too slowly!

waters, where the *Ameletus* is commonly found. The high-country version of this bug is unique in that it inhabits primarily lakes and tarns.

In the fall, when the *Ameletus* and *Siphlonurus* are done hatching, the third member of the trinity, the *Isonychia*, is just coming into its own. This is a truly gorgeous eggplant-colored nymph that leaves behind an incongruously orange husk when it molts. In the fall, you will find hundreds of these nymphal exoskeletons plastered to the downstream side of midstream boulders, looking for all the world like dried shrimp shells. Often they are mixed with the husks of emerging October caddis, which can be immediately identified by their sweeping antennae in contrast with the *Isonychia*'s tiny stubs. The adult has a rusty body and sports unmistakable tall, gray wings. On waters such as the Pit and the Klamath, *Isonychia* so dominate the hatch that anglers tossing giant orange Stimulators to imitate the obvious October caddis often walk away skunked, muttering something about how the fish weren't feeding.

If only they had darted a size 12 dark gray nymph through the shallows.

30
Grasshoppers and Crickets

Only mosquitoes rank above grasshoppers as the most economically devastating insects on the planet. In most areas of the world, plagues of locusts are of far greater concern than plagues of knife-wielding meth freaks or even bubonic plague. On the other hand, trout love grasshoppers and so do I.

Like stoneflies and mayflies, grasshoppers do not undergo a metamorphic pupal phase but mature through a series of nymphal stages. Baby hoppers are small, cute images of their adult selves without wings. As they mature and molt, each stage has increasingly well-developed wings and pectoral muscles. The mature adults in most species have large wings and are strong fliers. They are not strong swimmers.

Crickets are raised on a commercial scale for pet frog and lizard feed as well as for bait. You can mail-order crickets from places like the Top Hat Cricket Ranch ("Put our chirps in your herps") for something less than $15 per thousand. Like mail-order brides, these mail-order crickets are available in a variety of shapes and sizes. The fresh-hatched "pin heads" look like fleas, and their brethren can be ordered in eighth-inch increments up to the fully fledged one-inch adults.

I am the Jack Kevorkian of grasshoppers and crickets. Fish, Lisa, and I have assisted in the suicides (okay, murder) of literally thousands and thousands of the mail-order beasts. In various waters with scuba tanks on the stream- or lakebed and a leviathan weight belt draped across my lap, I have watched as Lisa tossed handfuls of crickets to waiting trout, whitefish, and smallmouth bass. Occasionally we have gone au naturel and used fresh-caught, organic, streamside grasshoppers instead of ranch crickets. I am thoroughly convinced that crickets and hoppers look and behave identically when tossed in the water, and fish don't have a clue whether they are dining on an Acrididae or a Gryllacrididae.

The Acrididae (grasshoppers) are diurnal insects that have small antennae and "sing" by scraping together specialized frictional areas between the hind leg and forewing. The Gryllacrididae (crickets) have long antennae, which help them navigate during their nocturnal sojourns, and produce song by scraping together the bases of the forewings. But from a trout's perspective, they are the same insect.

When a grasshopper hits the water, it apparently is stunned and remains motionless for a few seconds. Fish attuned to feeding on hoppers often zero in on the splat of the bug and slam it instantly. If the grab

grasshopper

The most important factor influencing a fish's willingness to eat hoppers is abundance. If hoppers are few, trout usually shun them.

isn't immediate, it probably won't happen until the hopper makes some sort of motion. Fly tiers and casual observers are quick to point out the importance of the long, powerful legs stabbing futilely into the water as the hopper tries to jump out of the river. I'm not nearly as convinced. I have removed the legs of hundreds of crickets, and they were eaten with no more or less abandon than their fully legged friends.

From my observations, which sometimes are not the same as what I've read or heard, the important factors governing hopper consumption are as follows:

The most important factor is abundance. If hoppers are not on the water or have not been on the water in the past few days, they won't get eaten. We have had trout and bass in our home aquarium that have become accustomed to eating goldfish, krill (floating and wet), or bloodworms. Drop in a couple of crickets and they will likely drown before getting consumed. After a day or two of feeding on crickets, the trout and bass will usually continue to eat them in preference to other, equally available foods.

On one less than memorable occasion, I needed to shoot a down-and-dirty video of trout eating hoppers from an underwater vantage. Unfortunately this was in February, and even if the rivers were open to fishing, snow hoppers were few and far between. We dialed up Top Hat Cricket Ranch, got a few thousand crickets, and road-tripped to the Green River below Flaming Gorge. The water was crystal clear, and hundreds of fat trout were rising to midges and blue-winged olives. For four days I sat in the water and froze my ass off. For four days Lisa patiently tossed crickets amid the noses of surface-feeding trout, and for four days we saw not a single trout eat a single cricket.

It was during this trip many years ago that Lisa perfected and considered patenting the Cricket Toss. Crickets and hoppers have quite clingy little feet and don't like getting thrown into rivers. To coax the little guys to let go of her fingers, she would hold them in an open fist, shake them like a pair of dice, and lob the dazed forms into the water with a straight-arm shooting motion. From afar, she looked as though she were playing cricket craps. I have four days of video of this technique if anyone is interested.

The next most important factor is motion. Trout will either snap up the cricket when it splashes onto the water or wait until the cricket starts moving. A cricket is a heavy-bodied terrestrial that sits low in the water. As it moves (kicks its feet, flaps its wings, picks its teeth, or whatever), its heavy body dips up and down, and deep ripples emanate from the hopper epicenter. It is these fat waves that attract fish, not the particular action of the bug.

To imitate this bobbing motion, do *not* skate, drag, or otherwise swim the fly. Trout will flee in terror. Raise your rod high in the air so that you create a nearly tight line between the rod tip and the hopper pattern. Deftly twitch the rod tip up and down a few times so that it nods the head of the fly. Don't overdo it; less is better than more.

The third most important factor is size. This one is way below abundance and motion (presentation) in importance, but the size of the hopper can make or break a selective fish. Toss a one-inch hopper amid a bunch of quarter-inch hoppers and it will likely as not be ignored. Try to match the size, but when in doubt, go smaller than the average hopper.

The fourth and least important factor is fly pattern. A well-presented Muddler Minnow works about as well as a buffed-out Dave's Hopper. My favorite hopper is Jack Gartside's Gartside Hopper, made of pulled-over elk hair (like an old-fashioned bullet-head bucktail streamer) and a wing of glued pheasant. Lisa prefers a Stimulator, because hopper season melds into October caddis season and the fly works equally well for both bugs. More often than not, I fish with Andy Burk's Spent Hopper, because he sells them to me for such a good deal, trout and smallies eat them like candy, and they look so cool!

Finally, if trout are giving your dry fly the cold shoulder, put a split shot on it and fish it wet. It isn't nearly as much fun, but even the most jaded trout can hardly turn up its nose at a drowned hopper served at mouth level.

31
Leeches

Leeches are like cats: Most with which I've had close relationships love me because I feed them.

During an exceptionally hard day's night, I collapsed to the sodden muck of a Malaysian rain forest floor, where I slept fitfully through the night. I awoke to a splitting headache and a severe case of nasal congestion. The headache was due to some wickedly wonderful jungle brew, and the congestion to a finger-size leech hanging out of my nostril. It wasn't one of the deadly thread leeches that burrow into the sinuses, but it made for an ugly morning nonetheless. My buddies thought it was awesome. One especially compassionate fly-fishing friend cracked, "That's one woolly booger!"

The fathers of modern surgery, barbers, used leeches to bleed their patients to rid them of everything from heart palpitations to scurvy. After each therapeutic bloodletting, the barber would hang his blood-soaked towels on a special white post to dry. Today's red-and-white striped barber poles are the modern icon of this past practice.

Barbers stopped using leeches when they became hairstylists—it was bad for the image. In their place, vascular surgeons have picked up the baton and today use leeches to remove pooled blood from resected limbs. Leeches are completely antiseptic, they don't transmit disease, and because of a natural anesthetic, the bite is absolutely painless. Except for HMO administrators, nothing in modern medicine can equal the leech for removing blood.

The problem with medicinal leeches is that they feed only every few months, and if they aren't in the mood, next to nothing will get them to eat. Ig Nobel Award–winning scientists Hogne Sandvik and Anders Baerheim did experiments with leeches to try to make them feed. The first experiment was to smear the patients with sour cream. The leeches were ambivalent.

Next they tried feeding the patients lots of garlic prior to exposing them to leeches. Vampires and garlic have gone hand in hand for centuries, so it only made sense to test the combination. In an amazing twist of fate, garlic-reeking humans indeed turned the recalcitrant leeches into feeding machines. Unfortunately, the pleasures of a garlic-flavored blood meal proved fatal to the leeches, and they died within hours of supper. For ethical reasons, the garlic trials were canceled.

The final experiment was to dunk leeches in beer (Guinness stout and Hansa bock) prior to letting them loose on their human hosts. Some of the drunk leeches got the munchies, but others (quote courtesy of the *Bri-*

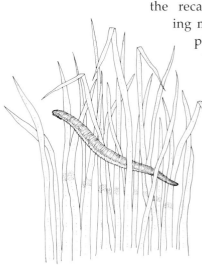

swimming leech

tish Medical Journal 309 (1994): 1689) "changed their behaviour, swaying their forebodies, losing grip and falling on their backs. . . . After having completed the first part of the study, the leeches became lazy and their scientific enthusiasm diminished. Discipline failed, appointments were forgotten and some even ran away on their own."

Like earthworms, to which they are closely related, leeches are hermaphroditic, sporting both male and female sexual organs, but try as they might, they are incapable of self-fertilization or self-regeneration. Amazon leeches rear their young inside their stomachs, but notably lax as parents, most common leeches simply dump their eggs into silk cocoons and leave them to the elements.

Baby leeches are born in the early spring and emerge from their cocoons a few weeks later. Fully equipped with thirty-two brains (seriously), two mouths, and a lust for life, they wander the waterways and moist terrestrial areas in search of food. Leeches are celebrated sanguivores (bloodsuckers), but most actually feed on small invertebrates, carrion, or even fish and amphibian eggs.

People generally think of leeches as dark ambassadors of the tropical underworld, but they inhabit waters across the globe. I have seen them in waters ranging from the skank of irrigation ditches to virtually sterile timberline tarns.

Most leeches are nocturnal and spend the daylight hours hidden under rocks or sticks or buried in mud. They emerge in low light to hunt for food. Some species are ambush predators and lie in wait for passing fare. Ambush leeches are commonly seen hanging suspended from the surface film by their posterior suckers. Often these bushwhackers get bushwhacked by hungry trout, which seem to relish the dangling forms. An unweighted Kaufmann's Mini Leech or Marabou Leech suspended from a well-greased tippet can wreak havoc with these trout.

The "best" leeches swim about looking for all the world like slowly fluttering ribbons. They look absolutely nothing like

The leech can inch along like a caterpillar, swim like a fluttering band of chamois, or cling like, well, a leech to the underside of the surface film and get transported by the wind. In any case, it's the rare trout that will turn up its nose at a leech.

Woolly Buggers or any of the other several dozen so-called "leech" patterns. My belief is that trout feed on actively stripped Woolly Buggers, Egg-Sucking Leeches, Electric Leeches, and the like simply because they look delicious. A true leech pattern would be a flat strip of soft leather hooked at one end with a small weight near the eye and s-l-o-w-l-y pulled through the water.

Uncle Josh has several incredible leech flies, but he calls them pork rind baits and sells them in units called Pigs in a Jar. They're heavy, but a 7-weight casts them well enough.

32
Mosquitoes

Admit it. One of your earliest forays into the world of matching the hatch led you to the mosquito bin. Long before you ever heard of mayflies, much less caddisflies, you knew mosquitoes on a blood-brother basis. It only made sense that when clouds of mosquitoes were dining on you, trout were dining on mosquitoes.

If only it were so simple.

Our pond is a run-of-the-mill California foothills pond. It is so generic that it could be used as the poster child for farm ponds. It is very similar to another pond that lies just on the other side of the ridge. On the winding dirt roads and ditch trails that separate these ponds, it takes about twenty minutes on my bike to connect the dots. To a mosquito aided by a soft breeze, unencumbered by the vagaries of irrigation needs or the engineering dynamics of road building, the lakes are only minutes apart.

Our pond is simply known as our pond. Its sister is known as Lake Vera. Lake Vera is the aquatic equivalent of the cow that burned down Chicago.

In the not-so-distant past, a man traveled to Lake Vera to camp on its shores under the cool shade of its cedars. He had recently returned from a trip to Korea, and plasmodium parasites had set up residence in his blood, where they frolicked about like tiny sea monkeys. One, or perhaps several, of Lake Vera's *Anopheles* mosquitoes spied the man and invited themselves to dinner.

The mosquito landed, apparently unnoticed, on a bare patch of the man's skin and commenced witching for blood. Its pair of cutting stylets lowered and immediately began sliding back and forth against each other like tiny electric knives. The knives effortlessly and painlessly sliced through his yielding skin with surgical precision. Through this slit, the mosquito inserted a tubelike fascicle bundled between the stylets. Like a fiber-optic, heat-seeking device, the fascicle probed beneath the skin searching for an arteriole from which to feed. When the mosquito didn't find a blood-rich vessel, it withdrew the fascicle and angled it in at another tangent. The mosquito repeated this probing until it found and tapped the mother lode. With each insertion of the fascicle, a tiny drop of anticoagulant was spilled into the opening of the wound to create a puddle of scab-resistant blood. The mosquito quickly finished its blood meal, withdrew its fascicle, and flew to the safety of a vertical perch, perhaps the bark of a cedar just behind the man's camp, from which to digest its dinner.

Assisted by gravity tugging at the mosquito's anus, the water quickly separated from the serum and left the mosquito with a gut packed with protein, platelets, and plasmodia. Within a month, three dozen kids at Lake Vera's Girl Scout camp had been bitten with plasmodium-infected mosquitoes. The girls dispersed to all corners of California, bringing home with them sunburned cheeks, skinned knees, and malaria.

Several hundred active cases of malaria are documented in California every year. In the coast range, the Sierra foothills, and especially the Central Valley, the malaria-carrying *Anopheles* mosquito is abundant. It would seem that we are under imminent threat of a malaria epidemic, but through tireless vigilance, the disease has a difficult time gaining a toehold in modern California, although historically malaria killed thousands throughout the state.

Malaria needs a reservoir of plasmodium-carrying hosts to maintain its existence. When a malaria outbreak occurs, patients are aggressively treated so that they can no longer transmit the disease, and area waters are attacked with insecticides, mosquito-killing bacteria, and hungry *Gambusia* minnows. *Anopheles* mosquitoes prefer rather large, clean bodies of water, so their breeding grounds are easily identified for treatment.

The new mosquito-borne kid on the block is the West Nile virus. Unlike malaria, West Nile virus does not require a human reservoir but exists quite nicely on many very mobile animals, including birds. To make matters better for the virus, it enjoys what is known as vertical transmission: The mother can infect her offspring without the aid of an intermediary host.

West Nile virus was first discovered in Uganda in the late 1930s. In 1999, it made landfall on our East Coast and spread across the continent with alarming speed. In 2003, it finalized the cross-country trip and settled into California.

Despite the hype, West Nile virus usually makes a more virulent media bite than a mosquito bite. After being bitten by a virus-carrying mosquito, most people will never know they got infected. About 20 percent of the victims will become sick with a range of flulike symptoms, and most will pass it off as a bad cold. One person in 150 will become very seriously ill with convulsions, coma, paralysis, and in some cases death. Of those who survive, a few will be burdened by neurological effects for the rest of their lives.

It *will* become a disease of fly fishers. West Nile virus is carried by the *Culex* mosquito. Unlike the *Anopheles,* which lives in the vicinity of warmer bass water, the *Culex* is ubiquitous and lives just about anywhere humans can; in fact, its common name is the house mosquito. It doesn't breed in open bodies of water, but instead prefers small, murky pockets of water such as found in tree holes, discarded tires, and those swampy backwaters adjacent to every trout stream. *Culex* is the living incarnation of the mosquito in your fly box.

I have had the privilege to work, live, and fish in some of the most notorious mosquito terrain in the world. From the tundra to the tropics, I've experienced mosquito densities that warp the imagination; yet I honestly believe the wet-year swarms in our very own Sierra rival that of any place on earth.

Will West Nile virus render our trout waters uninhabitable to fly fishers? I would certainly hope no one would be so paranoid as to stop fishing after sunset. But in a country where people wrap their homes in plastic and duct tape during a "Code Orange," and the media turn every case into a circus event, nothing would surprise me. Back East, where the virus has taken up residence, entire neighborhoods go quiet at dusk as people retreat indoors behind the safety of window screens and glass.

Common sense should tell you not to hide in the house, but roll down your sleeves, slather on the insect repellent, and go fishing. DEET has been a proven repellent since World War II, and its use has been studied ruthlessly. Any repellent containing more than 34 percent DEET should be avoided. It has been shown over and over and over again that if a mosquito is not repelled at 34 percent, it will not be repelled at 100 percent. Also, 100 percent DEET degrades as quickly as 34 percent DEET, so a triple dose is not three times more effective or effective for three times as long. The stuff doesn't chase bugs away; it simply confuses their ability to perceive you as prey. The greater the concentration of DEET, the greater the concentration that will be absorbed into your skin—never a good idea. And the higher the concentration, the greater the likelihood of it damaging your fly line, plastic watch face, or clothing. Some of the new time-release DEET formulations seem to work as promised and can provide up to twelve hours of protection.

The mosquito needs no introduction; its irritating bite can sometimes be the prelude to a nasty illness. Despite their prevalence near trout waters, mosquitoes rarely make themselves available to fish, and to the trout a mosquito imitation probably represents a midge.

Citronella, fern juice, niacin, Skin-So-Soft, and other "alternative" repellents are comparatively ineffective. It would certainly be nice if, like the SPF rating of sunblocks, mosquito repellent could be rated against a commonly accepted set of standards. Sales of 100 percent DEET and alternative repellents would crumble.

Permethrin, a synthetic version of pyrethrum, a chrysanthemum extract, works very well when applied to clothing. By combining the repellent properties of DEET to your skin and the "knock-down" properties of permethrin to your clothes, you can obtain close to 100 percent protection against mosquito bites.

What are mosquitoes good for? Mostly, mosquitoes are good for making more mosquitoes. They certainly aren't any good for fishing with. Mosquitoes live near, but not in, trout water, so the fish never acquire a taste for the damn things. The trout that eat your mosquito imitation are probably mistaking it for a midge.

And just when you thought you had the hatch thing figured out.

33
Net-Spinning Caddisflies

A single family of caddisflies creates nearly half of all fishable hatches: Hydropsychidae or, more simply, the net spinners. In *The Caddisfly Handbook*, Carl Richards writes, "This is by far the most important caddisfly for trout fishermen." I would go one step further and say that this is one of the most important of *all insects* for trout fishermen to recognize and understand. But despite their immense importance, these caddis are one of the least understood and poorly replicated flies in the box. Almost no one fishes them effectively.

Hydropsychids are one of the few types of caddis that do not move about their environment in search of food. Instead, the net spinners build web retreats and let the food come to them. They build gorgeous funnel-shaped silken traps or span seines across gaps between rocks and sticks. The nets are so predictably symmetrical that it has been suggested that anomalies in the weave can be used to detect certain water pollutants that interfere with the bugs' ability to spin.

Psychotropic drugs have a similar effect on spider behavior. Spiders fed flies laced with mescaline weave neat intricate designs, and those fed LSD spin outrageous webs with long spiking cusps. On the other hand, a little bit of caffeine screws them up so badly that they build nets that can barely hold themselves together, much less catch insects.

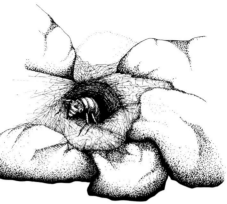

caddis larva in net

Four genera of Hydropsychidae are of major importance to North American anglers: *Arctopsyche, Hydropsyche, Cheumatopsyche, and Macronema.*

Arctopsyche dwell in headwater creeks and streams. This caddis weaves a wide mesh net suited for passing gravel and the large grains of sand found in its alpine habitat. It is a large caddisfly that spends two years in the larval stage. Its size and year-round presence combined with a propensity to drift make it a familiar food item to trout in almost any mountain stream. You can never go wrong drifting a size 4 to 8 olive-colored caddis larva under a couple of split shot.

Hydropsyche runs head-to-head with *Glossosoma* as being the most abundant caddis in the majority of our freestone trout waters. Unlike the *Glossosoma*, which hides inside clumps of rocks, is very small, and usually has a single brood per year, the uncased *Hydropsyche* is continuously exposed to trout, is of respectable size (ranging from size 8 to 16), and can cycle through two or more generations in a fishing season. According to Gary LaFontaine, "*Hydropsyche* is the most important caddisfly in America."

Despite the fact that *Hydropsyche* builds a web retreat, it frequently strays and is commonly found roaming about the

This rock is covered by the cup-shaped nets of Hydropsyche. *It is not uncommon to see this kind of abundance across an entire riverbed.*

streambed, draping strands of silk behind it in the cobbles. The silk not only works as a leash should the larvae lose its footing, but it also is used by the caddis as a rappel line to lower itself across gaps between the rocks.

The larvae are earth-toned and difficult to see against the streambed background. By contrast, the silk strands almost glow and are easily visible from a distance. Trout have learned to key in on this luminescent line and frequently graze on the silk lines whether they have attached larvae or not. You can lighten the tippet for a foot or so above the larva imitation with a white grease pen, such as a Mean Streak marker, to clue trout in to the idea something edible might be drifting their way.

When it comes time for pupation, the *Hydropsyche* entombs itself inside a dome of gravel. If you peel one of these domes off the face of a boulder, you'll see that the bottom of the gravel dome is a sheet of silk through which you can view the evolving pupa. With exception of the *Rhyacophila*, all other caddis pupae will be completely surrounded with sand or gravel.

Hydropsyche *larvae are perpetually tethered to the streambed by strands of silk. Even when the larvae are camouflaged, the silk threads give away their positions.*

The larva has secured itself inside a gravel shelter and is about to commence pupation.

Pupation lasts for a few weeks to more than a month. Emergence takes place in the early morning or late afternoon. During hot periods, it may not occur until dark. The pupa chews a hole at the end of its gravel chamber and shimmies out. At this point it is a fully formed adult encased in a thin, plasticlike membrane with a pair of long swimming legs. Technically, it is no longer a pupa but a *pharate adult*. The pupa (pharate adult is too much of a mouthful to repeat) drifts along the streambed anywhere from a few feet to more than a hundred yards. While it drifts, the pupa hangs motionless as air is generated between the insect and its husk. During strong periods of emergence, trout hover atop the streambed to feed on drifting pupae rather than making the effort to surface feed. A Bird's Nest or LaFontaine Deep Sparkle Pupa dead drifted into these fish is the key to success. At this stage, most fish won't bother swimming after a swinging fly.

After a period of drift, the pupa kicks into gear and starts swimming with its long, paddlelike swimmerets. Anyone who has watched a back swimmer or water boatman pumping through the water will have a very good picture of how a swimming caddisfly pupa behaves. Assisted by buoyant gases that have developed within the cuticle, it ascends to the surface, where it once again goes into an acquiescent state and drifts immediately under the film. As in its bottom drift, it will float for a few feet or many yards before kicking into action a second time and breaking through the film to emerge.

The pupae are strong and agile swimmers that will dodge and dart to avoid trout. Explosive or splashy rises are a strong indication that trout are chasing down swimming pupae. Bulging rises are usually caused by trout feeding on the pupae that are quietly drifting under the film. In splashy situations, swim, swing, or lift your fly; I like a Bird's Nest or soft-hackle. With bulging rises, a drag-free drift is usually mandatory, because trout are looking at the silhouette of the dark fly against a relatively bright sky, and any sort of drag is translated into a telltale wake on the surface. Here I use a Bird's Nest or unweighted LaFontaine Pupa hung in the film underneath a greased leader.

Emergence is normally rapid. Caddis wings are kept dry inside the cuticle and are coated with dense hairs that avoid wetting. I have seen *Hydropsyche* that stretched their wings and rode the water for a few seconds before taking wing, but usually a quick flutter or twitch is the only preamble to flight. Trout rarely key on these emerging adults.

Caddisflies are less prone than mayflies to getting trapped in their shucks during emergence; however, even a 5 percent entrapment rate equates to thousands of crippled insects during a strong hatch. Unlike crippled mayflies, which invariably die within minutes of their aborted emergence, caddis are durable, long-lived insects that can survive for days partially trapped in their pupal exuviae. These crippled caddis can feed, drink, and spend the rest of their unfortunate lives in the shadows behind boulders, under alders, or helplessly caught in eddies, going round, round, and round.

Emergent crippled caddis are a familiar and frequent food item. Unlike most other bugs, which are available at specific times, these caddis are encountered almost anywhere in the trout stream at all times of day throughout the season. Without even a close second, my favorite searching pattern is the E/C (Emergent Crippled) Caddis, which was developed over several years to imitate this most vulnerable stage.

The adult *Hydropsyche* spend a few days or even weeks feeding, mating, and otherwise cavorting in the riparian vegetation. In the evening, enthusiastic mating swarms appear like smoke just above the tops of streamside plants. These swirling orgies don't necessarily equate with ovipositing or emergence, and it is common to have caddis on the wing but none available in the water.

The fertilized female crawls or swims to the streambed to lay strings of green or yellow eggs on the subsurface boulders. Air bubbles cling to her hairy wings and body, and the caddis breathes off this coat of bubbles, called a plastron. As she consumes the oxygen, the partial pressures between the water and bubbles force fresh oxygen into the plastron. The female can stay underwater indefinitely but is normally done ovipositing in less than an hour. A Bird's Nest treated with a desiccant fly floatant perfectly imitates the air-encrusted ovipositor. Some fish will feed only on flies drifted without drag along the streambed; others seem to be triggered by the sight of a glittering Bird's Nest being lifted or swung though the water like a swimming adult caddis.

When the caddis is done laying her eggs, she lets go of the streambed and allows the buoyant plastron to lift her to the surface. Once on the surface, she'll skitter to shore or drift exhausted with wings splayed out across the film. Most *Hydropsyche* oviposit a single time, but they have the ability to return to the streambed up to three times. There are many spent caddis patterns, but I think a partridge soft-hackle is pretty hard to beat.

Cheumatopsyche and *Macronema* are, for all intents and purposes, just a smaller version of the *Hydropsyche*. The common name for the *Cheumatopsyche* is little sister sedge (not to be confused with Sister Sledge), in apparent comparison with her big sister, *Hydropsyche*. *Cheumatopsyche* prefers warmer and slower waters than her big sister's habitat and is often found in downstream reaches that are only marginally supportive of trout.

34
Scuds

Eons ago, my good friend John Marcacci and I drove to the Green River for a day's fishing. It was back in the time when it didn't seem remarkable that three days of driving would net only ten hours of fishing. This was before they invented designated drivers and getting there was half the fun.

We were having so much fun getting there that, at oh-dark-thirty on a dirt road in the middle of the Utah desert, it didn't seem relevant that we were passing official-looking U.S. government signs suggesting we immediately stop and turn around. It didn't even seem too relevant that a very sturdy gate blocked the road. We simply four-wheeled onto some railroad tracks and kept on truckin'. At that point, the only thing that mattered was that the ice chest wasn't quite empty and we were heading south toward great fishing. We thought we were going east.

We must have pulled over to take a nap, because the next thing I remember I was waking up feeling ill. I blamed it on the gorgeous black widow spider that dropped out of my sleeping bag. John was actively getting sick, but since he didn't sleep with a spider, he could only blame the cheap beer.

The truck was sandwiched between heaps of what looked like rusted missiles with jagged holes blasted out of their sides. Between retches, John suggested they were drones used for navy target practice. Pitched in the sand, skeletal railroad tank cars with "ANTHRAX" stenciled on their flanks hulked silently, as spindrifts of snow and alkaline dust swirled through their rotting carcasses. We were in a military junkyard.

We built a small cooking fire from a pile of eight-foot railroad ties and brewed some much-needed coffee. While sipping the joe, we tied flies by the warmth of the fire some forty feet away. We had been told that the only thing Green River trout ate was scuds. Neither of us had ever seen a scud before, but armed with a Herter's catalog, we copied the pattern from its dog-eared pages.

We bent the hooks, dubbed scraggly bodies, added a few wraps of mallard flank, pulled strips of plastic over the backs, and ribbed them with light wire, just like many modern scud patterns. After tying a few that looked like the picture, our hands were trembling so badly (was it the cold, the beer, or the anthrax?) that we couldn't grip the plastic, so we omitted that step. Pretty soon we decided that since we didn't need to tie down the plastic, we might as well save time and not tie in the wire either.

We finally got to the river and could only stare, goggle-eyed, at all the really cool trout finning in the very cool water just below our extremely cold feet. We kicked over a few rocks, and clouds of scuds billowed into the current, where the trout eagerly darted to and fro feasting on the bounty. It was just like the wild rumors we had heard in California, except that the fish didn't want our flies.

After a juniper reached out and stole his fly on a backcast, John tied on another scud and suddenly started catching fish. I watched closely and made sure he wasn't dipping his flies in Dr. Juice or tipping his scuds with caddis larvae. He was being uncharacteristically kosher. I asked what he was doing differently, and he shrugged his shoulders, smiled smugly, and said wisely, "I dunno."

Just to be doubly sure he wasn't smearing just a little Powerbait on the fly, I offered to help him release his next fish. As we were unhooking the trout, we both realized that he had tied on one of the flies without plastic or wire. It was just greenish dubbing with a wrap of duck flank . . . very similar to a Bird's Nest, except that we didn't know what those were back then.

I scooped up some of the living scuds and watched as they scurried about in the diminishing puddle of water in my hand. They nuzzled into the darkness between my fingers, and I learned two important lessons about scuds. First of all, swimming scuds, the kind fish are likely to see, are as straight as a needle; they curl up into the typical scud-fly profile only when they are crawling around on something. The second lesson I learned was that I liked these little guys.

Since then, I've spent an embarrassing number of hours underwater observing scuds and watching fishermen try to trick fish into eating scuds. For those moments I can't be on the water, we have an aquarium in our kitchen that has become home to countless generations of scuds.

Like crayfish, shrimp, and sow bugs, scuds are crustaceans. They belong to the order Amphipoda, which contains three families. *Gammarus* and *Hyalella* are the families of greatest importance to fly fishers. Like insects, scuds periodically shed their exoskeletons, but unlike insects, scuds don't have nymphal or pupal stages. Baby scuds look like their adult counterparts, only cuter.

Scuds require a relatively large amount of calcium to support their molts. They are found almost exclusively in alkaline waters, and wherever they are found, trout actively seek out these nutrient-rich packets of energy. In scud-rich waters such as Thompson Valley Reservoir or Eagle Lake, I've seen trout bellies distended by *hundreds* of scuds. To offset such intense predation, scuds are remarkably prolific.

Fairy shrimp are often confused with scuds. Typically, fairy shrimp dwell in quiet pools and puddles outside of trout habitat.

When river levels abruptly drop, scuds frequently are stranded and die. In death, they turn as bright orange as boiled shrimp. When the water rises again, the rivers are chummed with orange scuds, and trout quickly key on them to the exclusion of everything else.

Scud populations have been measured as dense as ten thousand creatures per cubic meter of water. A single pair can spawn half a dozen times in a year and produce twenty thousand young. The single largest threat to scud populations is the rapid drawdown of tailwaters below dams. On one scud-laden Truckee River tributary, it is common to find windrows of dead and dying scuds when the river flow is abruptly cut. These normally light olive scuds turn bright orange when they die, and trout in this creek are quite color selective when flow patterns change.

Scuds are generally reported to be herbivores and scavengers. Our pets are vicious predators. They will dart from cover to attack tubefix worms and will even tackle small back swimmers, which themselves are pretty lethal creatures. Scuds can easily overpower *Siphlonurus* mayfly nymphs sevenfold their weight, and we have witnessed scuds, sometimes in groups, attacking and killing tadpoles.

Though scuds live in the shallowest margins of lakes and streams, they intensely dislike light. They typically hide in deep cover while the sun is shining but quickly come out to forage when the skies dim. I've watched fish boiling through masses of scuds as they rose out of elodea mats when afternoon cumulus clouds melted shadows across the lake. As soon as the sun broke through the clouds, the scuds would vanish and the melee would cease. Under overcast skies, scud patterns very often outfish "normal" nymph and pupa patterns.

swimming scuds

A scud crawls over a rock searching for bits of food. Trout normally see swimming scuds, which are not curled like the standard imitations but are straight as an arrow.

The scud has seven pairs of legs; the first two are used for grasping and manipulation, and the other five propel the bug with synchronous ripples. When swimming, the scud stretches out completely straight; this is why curved scud patterns not only look wrong when stripped through the water, but also have poor hooking ability. The scud bends into its characteristic curled position when it scuttles about along the streambed or among the vegetation.

When a scud swims, it becomes a blur of buzzing legs, whisking antennae, and fluttering gills; it travels upside down as often as not. There is no such thing as a good scud imitation. Don't even try to fool an educated fish into believing your hunk of Visqueen and feathers is the real thing. The occasional trout might eat it, but only because he's greedy.

Instead of trying to make a scud imitation, make a scud *impression*. Give the trout something that moves and twitches and doesn't have an up or a down or a sideways. Give them something simple like a Bird's Nest. Something that can be tied with frozen fingers on a military waste site in the morning after a forgotten night.

35

Snails

Beetles Rule

About a decade ago, Lisa and I made a whirlwind tour of the western spring creeks. From the mighty Henry's Fork to secret seeps trickling through private pastures, we visited them all. Before assaulting each water, we cruised the appropriate websites, talked with resident guides, and perused the local fly shops. The responses were typical and expected: Beetles rule.

The general consensus was that beetles were the fly of flies. One could expect Tricos, a few PMDs, some caddis, and hoppers for sure, but for a daylong predictably good time, beetles were the ticket.

In Livingston: "You will *need* beetles about noon when the fish start getting fussy." In West Yellowstone: "The beetle hatch is in full swing—be prepared." In Dillon: "Beetles are outfishing everything including hoppers right now." In Burney: "Here, take a few of these foam beetles; the fish are keyed in on them." A young and earnest guide on the banks of Silver Creek: "The trout are *feasting* on beetles. You can run your hand along their bellies and feel that they are gorged with them. They'll hardly eat anything else."

During our expedition, we dutifully rolled rocks, seined the drift, shook bugs out of bushes, and got on our hands and knees to tally the local bug demographics. We averaged maybe half a dozen beetles per creek per day. At Silver Creek, where the trout were "feasting on beetles," we found two. If the trout were holding out for their beetle fix, they should have been pretty damn scrawny and in full-blown detox.

I dove underwater to observe firsthand the effect of beetle withdrawals. In creek after creek, I slipped into the wet and sipped off the snorkel or regulator while I waited and watched. Despite the obvious lack of beetles, the trout seemed quite fat and docile. The occasional fish would rise to grasshoppers, but most were content to wait until a drowned hopper drifted into them at eye level. All in all, it was a pretty lazy scene.

While I shivered below, Lisa was having a fine time splatting Burk's Spent Hoppers tight to the banks. She could have caught more fish hanging the fly under a split shot but opted for the less frequent but supremely satisfying bassy surface takes. One of her fish ducked into an undercut and escaped but in the process was able to hang the fly among the roots. As Lisa waded across the creek to untangle her hopper, the shoals of indolent trout suddenly exploded.

At first I thought the fish were terrified, but then I realized they were in a feeding frenzy. Like crazed sharks, they shot back and forth across the current to take stuff dislodged by Lisa's wading. I pulled myself closer and saw that they were hammering fingernail-size black snails. Even after Lisa's chum trail dissipated, the fish continued slamming down snails. They pried them off the riverbed cobbles and stripped them off the dense aquatic grasses. I had been watching trout pluck snails from the drift, but only after I started actually watching for them did I realize just how many snails were either drifting with the flow or hanging under the surface film.

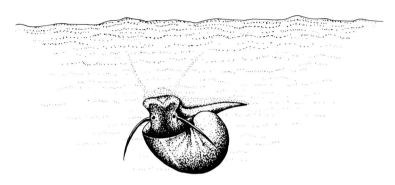

snail drifting on surface tension

Out of curiosity, Lisa tossed out a beetle pattern, and just like the guides said would happen, it got slammed. From below, the "beetle" imitation passed as a real-enough-looking floating snail to get bit.

Snails are a huge packet of food. Combine their nutritional value with the incredible numbers in which they inhabit trout waters, and it's no wonder fish actively seek them out. These gastropods are most susceptible to trout as they drift. The snail generates a bubble of air inside its shell, which buoys it to the surface. There the snails are dispersed by the movement of current and wind. Drifting snails can create dense mats on the downwind edges of lakes. The snail has an adhesive foot that allows it to actually crawl about on the underside of the rubbery surface film so that it can eat the algae and plankton that concentrate there.

From my underwater observation, a trout's perspective, snails appear in two distinctly different forms. Backlit by the sun, a drifting snail with a gas-filled shell appears soft and glows amber. Right beside it might be a snail crawling on the film, which appears quite opaque with a very hard silhouette. The most outstanding feature of a film-feeding snail is its foot. The foot, which is usually a brown, putty, or red color, pulls down the surface film, creating a light-condensing lens that results in a bright glow around the dark snail.

I don't know if trout prefer one snail over another, but I have developed a single pattern that seems to cover both bases. This pattern is in the running for the world's easiest—and possibly ugliest—fly. Wrap several layers of translucent brown "ice" chenille to form a ball on the forward half of a 2XL hook (Tiemco 5262 is my choice). At the eye of the hook, wrap a grizzly and furnace hackle several times to make a dense "foot." Done.

From underwater, the translucent chenille glows just right, and the hackle pulls down the film and creates that shimmery halo. The Cutter's Snail is a scientifically concocted imitation that has taken years to perfect. Any old beetle pattern probably works just as well.

36
Stoneflies

Stoneflies are an act of God; I'm sure if one cracked your windshield the insurance company would claim so.

How could anything *evolve* into a stonefly? They got the way they are eons before the most primitive dinosaur took its first baby step, and then they stopped changing. Then again, maybe they *did* change over and again only to be plucked off the evolutionary growth chart between the calloused thumb and forefinger of Mother Nature. Whether evolved or created, stoneflies are proof that the Peter Principal doesn't exist in the real world. Stoneflies are survivors.

I got to pondering stonefly evolution one summer evening while lying on my belly in the Madison River watching giant salmonfly (*Pteronarcys*) nymphs lumber into the shallows, their movements ponderous and plodding, as they prepared to hatch. One after another, these beasts would crawl up the slippery slope of a granite boulder, lose their footing in the swift current, and get swept downstream. Many got swept away while in plain

Stoneflies have lived, unchanged, since long before the first dinosaur roamed the earth. PHOTO BY MICHELLE MAHOOD

view of a following bug that never broke stride on its path to oblivion.

I let go of my rock and drifted downstream alongside the nymphs. They didn't swim for safety or drift across current lanes. They didn't fall to the streambed like heavily weighted sinkers. In fact, they didn't do much of anything at all except curl into a semifetal position and give themselves over to the mercy of the river. They rose in the upwellings, sank in the down drafts, and swirled in the eddies like the helpless, almost neutrally buoyant bugs that they are. Only when they passively approached some sort of solid ground did they uncurl and reach out for safety.

The behavior of the naturally drifting nymph is impossible to imitate with a standard lead-wrapped stonefly pattern. Weighted nymphs plunge to the streambed with slack in the line, and with the slightest bit of tension, they jink upwards or drag across the current in a decidedly unnatural way. By now you should know that presentation is far more important than a fly's shape, size, color, or silhouette. The best way to present a stonefly nymph is to use an *unweighted* imitation and add enough split shot to the tippet to keep the fly somewhere near the bottom.

Depending on species, stoneflies can live from one to three years in the nymphal state. Unlike the vast majority of aquatic trout foods, stonefly nymphs are available year-round in a variety of sizes. It is one of the few patterns that you can defend using 24/7. When the giant "glamour" bugs like the salmonfly and golden stone are ovipositing and available to fish, trout frequently still prefer the nymphs to the adults. Even adult stonefly patterns sunk with split shot are usually more readily taken than the dries. Unfortunate but true.

Some stonefly nymphs can swim, but the motion is a feeble side-to-side wriggling that lacks impetus or enthusiasm. Imagine a fat lady doing the hula in a geriatric therapy pool. Despite what you may have read elsewhere, stonefly nymphs cannot swim to the surface and hatch like mayflies.

Little yellow stoneflies (*Isoperla*) are rumored to emerge through the film like mayflies, and I helped perpetuate that myth in *Sierra Trout Guide*. I read about it in supposedly well-respected fishing literature, and to my unquestioning eyes they sure *looked* like they were hatching out of the water. After *Trout Guide* was published, I was forced to look at the stonefly "hatch" with a more critical eye. The world's preeminent stonefly expert (and good friend) Dr. Richard Baumann called me up and patiently explained in detail how it was physically impossible for this phenomenon to take place.

A few years later while fishing on the Truckee, I ran a seine across the film to see what the fish were rising to. In the net I found the usual assortment of aquatic insects, including a large contingent of adult little yellow stoneflies. What I *didn't* find were any stonefly shucks. There were plenty of mayfly nymph shucks and caddis pupae exuviae but none of the shucks that should have accompanied the ongoing little yellow stone "hatch."

Subsequent observations both above and below water confirmed what Dr. Baumann said and what the seine indicated—stonefly nymphs were not swimming to the surface to emerge. Instead, ovipositing adults were getting stuck in the film where they were virtually impossible to see from an angler's perspective. They would drift unnoticed, sometimes for hundreds of feet, and then with one quick burst of energy would launch into the air. Frequently they would skip once or twice before actually taking flight.

In the slowest sections of river, the little yellow stone adults would launch from the water at any angle to the current, but in quicker reaches, they seemed to prefer launching upstream. To imitate that behavior, make a downstream presentation, let it drift drag-free, and then give a brief twitch or skip upstream and let it drift some more. Even though a flush floating pattern such as a CDC caddis looks more appropriate on the water than a high riding model, a well-hackled, clipped deer-hair body rides lighter and makes a much more convincing skip. I'd love for you to run out and buy a bushel of Cutter's Little Yellow Stoneflies, but to be truthful, an Elk Hair Caddis treated with powdered fly floatant probably works just about as well.

To solidify the conclusion that little yellow stones don't emerge midstream, Lisa and I spent several summers rearing various stoneflies in an eight-foot-long "bug tank." When given a stick or rock to crawl out and hatch from, the stones did great; when the vehicles for escape were removed, 100 percent of the nymphs drowned while attempting to molt into the adult stage 100 percent of the time.

adult stonefly landing on branch

Once the nymph crawls out of the water and molts, the winged adult immediately seeks refuge in streamside vegetation, where it rocks out. Both males and females of many species are awesome drummers. They beat the ends of their abdomens against the stage upon which they're performing in a rhythmic series of taps and pauses like Morse code. The code is species-specific and is assumed to be a method of courtship or mate-finding. I'm not kidding.

In comparison with most other aquatic insects, stoneflies are poor fliers. Perhaps because of their relative inability to easily disperse across watersheds, regional differences in habits can be profound. In some watersheds, *Pteronarcys* nymphs hatch into adults a few hours after sunset, but in other waters, the same species will hatch midmorning.

When threatened, instead of flying away, stoneflies usually drop deep into the foliage. If they happen to be on willows or alders overhanging a stream, this dash for refuge only puts them into the mouths of hungry trout. Fish *expect* to see stoneflies under alders. An imitation drifted downstream or skip-cast under vegetation usually gets blasted.

Stoneflies don't seem to have much going for them, but what do I know? Long after the last human being has flamed out, more than likely, stoneflies will just keep doing what they do best. Surviving.

37

Threadfin Shad

The coming of winter spells different things to different fly fishers. To some, winter means steelheading on the North Pacific coast; to others, it means drifting tiny midges on foothill tailwaters; and to still others, winter simply means it's time to hang up the rods until next spring. To me, late fall and winter mean stripers on the San Francisco Delta, and stripers on the delta mean shad.

Like the striped bass, the threadfin shad is an exotic species introduced from waters on the wrong side of the Rockies. In its native waters, the shad is recognized as an incredibly important forage item. Biologist Wayne Gustaveson writes that "all game-fish seem to prefer eating shad to the exclusion of anything else except maybe crayfish." In 1953, the California Department of Fish and Game imported several hundred threadfin from the Tennessee River and introduced them to waters in San Diego County. The San Diego bass responded with fantastic growth rates, and fisheries managers around the state clamored for the

Shad are the preferred forage fish in any water they share with predators. They travel in large schools, have a high fat content, and apparently taste good.

little fish. Shad were planted in impoundments of the Sacramento and San Joaquin watersheds and soon filtered throughout the system. Today they are found from Humboldt Bay to San Diego, and just as in their home waters, they have evolved into the food item of choice among California's game species.

The threadfin shad (*Dorosoma petenense*) is not to be confused with that popular gamefish the American shad. The American shad grows to five pounds, spends most of its life in the ocean, and eagerly gives fly rodders a run for their money. The threadfin grows to a maximum of six inches, lives its entire life in fresh or slightly brackish water, and rarely takes you into the backing.

The threadfin shad is named for an elegant fin ray that trails like a thread from the base of the dorsal fin to the wrist of the tail. The belly fins are translucent lemon yellow, and the back is metallic blue-green. The body is shaped like an elongated silvery coin, and almost dead center in the thorax is a distinct black spot that resembles a cigarette burn. The spot is used as a visual cue to keep schools intact.

Shad are highly prolific, and a single female can produce upward of twenty thousand eggs. Spawning occurs in the spring and summer. The female swims close to the surface, generally in a protected bay or at least out of the main body of a lake or river, followed by a cadre of three, four, or perhaps half a dozen suitors. Thousands of shad can spawn at the same time.

In May and July, large spawning schools are frequently encountered in San Luis, Oroville, and Millerton Lakes. In the delta, spawning starts as early as April near the Pittsburg and Contra Costa power plants, perhaps encouraged by the warm-water discharge, and I've seen spawning as late as August along the Walnut Grove bridge abutments.

As eggs are released, the males ejaculate into the stream of flowing ova, and then the parental duties are done. The eggs are extremely sticky and adhere to submerged rocks and stumps, as well as floating vegetation. Survival seems to be highest for eggs glued to a fixed item, but in reservoirs that fluctuate and leave fixed eggs high and dry, the floating eggs win. All in all it is a good reproductive strategy.

The eggs hatch in three to six days, and the shad larvae become a part of the plankton pool. As the larvae grow, they develop diel migration patterns, ascending to the surface at light and then dropping to lower depths at night. Growth is rapid, and by the end of August the young shad have developed schooling tendencies. The schools migrate into the open waters of impoundments, and in the delta they pool in vast numbers between Antioch and the Clifton Forebay. By late fall, the great schools disperse, and shad are most frequently found adjacent to dense weeds and in brushy coves.

Young shad are primarily filter feeders; they seine microscopic zooplankton and protozoa from the water and suck detritus from the rocks and weeds. At about four inches, they convert to a more cosmopolitan diet and consume phytoplankton, fish larvae, and small invertebrates.

The threadfin convert their food into a rich, oily flesh. Schools of shad can frequently be identified by the oil slick excreted by their numbers. In nervous water, the oil creates islands of tranquility as it flattens the riffles. In calm water, the oil produces a distinctive gloss. If the shad are running close to the surface, they create a shoal of nervous water that immediately brings an attending flock of whirling gulls, terns, and anglers.

Nothing is more effective at mashing a herd of threadfin than the striped bass. Stripers will run through a school of shad, slashing back and forth, grabbing mouthfuls of the bait as they flee in violent silvery clouds. When possible, shad will run into thick cover. It is common to see the water boil with shad inside tule jungles while fat wakes announce the presence of stripers patrolling the water just outside. In open water, shad spray into the air as marauding stripers slash at their heels. Terns and gulls welcome the airborne meals with open beaks. The most fun is when bass have shad pressed against a shore. The hapless little fish have nowhere to go but on the bank. Lisa and I spent one winter evening transfixed as shoal after shoal of shad tossed themselves against a delta riprap. Like shattered mirrors come to life, shad writhed and flipped amid the rocks in a futile attempt to dodge the gnashing jaws of Mother Nature. Stripers blitzed the schools, gulls whirled and dived overhead, and on the levee, herons, egrets, crows, raccoons, and crabs raced back and forth to grab the stranded shad. We cheered the mayhem with upraised bottles of wine and ignored our fly rods leaning against the gunwales. Compassion has its seasons.

Shad have high metabolic needs and rarely, if ever, stop feeding. I've caught shad in my throw nets and am continually amazed at how they begin to feed within minutes of being hauled from the water and unceremoniously dumped in a bait bucket or livewell. During a striper blitz, it is common to observe shad pecking on the confetti of glittering scales left by their stricken brothers. When an incoming tide is crawling up delta banks or whitecaps are crashing against a lakeshore, shad will shoal in mere inches of water as they crowd in to feed on the dislodged tidbits of food. As the tides pull away from the banks, shad will move, sometimes hundreds of yards in a few minutes,

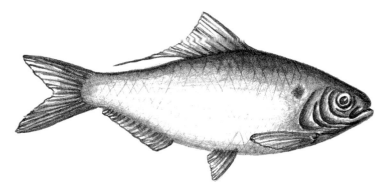

threadfin shad

to feed against banks parallel with the outgoing flow or set up in the mixing zones where they can inhale detritus caught in the currents.

Predators follow prey. On an incoming tide or wave-lapped lakeshore, cast tight to or parallel with the shore or tule break. This is prime time to work the backside of bays, scallops, and dead-end sloughs. On an outgoing tide, fish the cuts or just downcurrent of scouring flows.

Generally any familiar baitfish pattern will work if put near shad-feeding bass. My personal favorite is a Clouser Minnow, but deceivers, whistlers, zonkers, and Z-Minnows all have their advocates. Though shad are silvery light-colored fish, as a rule silvery light-colored flies aren't my first choice. As in trout fishing, I like dark imitations in dark conditions and lighter imitations under bright skies and clean water. If you were to allow me only one color when fishing stripers, it would be chartreuse, which seems to work well in all conditions.

Sometimes a zillion shad can be too much of a good thing. When stripers key exclusively on shad, like spring-creek trout rising to spinners, the bass become highly suspicious of flies that don't look and act perfect. Some of the most difficult delta fishing to be had is at night under dock lights, where shad congregate and bass feed on nothing but shad. Allowing lightly weighted deceivers and zonkers to flutter through the schools is often better than trying to imitate a swimming shad.

When bass are busting a big school of bait and birds are twirling overhead, sometimes it is all but impossible to provide a credible imitation. In these situations, sometimes a gurgler, balsa slider, or popper jerked quickly away from the war zone will invoke the strike of a bass enticed more by the action of a wounded baitfish than the actual imitation itself. It is also in these situations that you'll often find the biggest, baddest bass lying beneath the frenzy rather than taking part. A Clouser fished deep will sometimes connect with a bruiser when all surface stuff is ignored or taken only by twenty-pound dinks.

38

Winter Stoneflies

Today, as I write this piece, it's Superbowl Sunday, and this afternoon I'm going fishing. It is one of the few times I can visit my secret spot and be assured I won't be bothered by dozens of other people who mistakenly consider this *their* secret spot. I'm going to cast my favorite rod, stand on my favorite secret rock, and fish with my favorite Superbowl fly. By the time the game is over, I will have experienced the finest day of trout fishing so far this year. Odds are in my favor, because it will be my first day of trout fishing this year.

I won't tell you about my favorite rod because you don't care. I won't tell you about my favorite secret rock because all my friends will care. I will instead tell you about the only bug that you need to imitate when fishing on Superbowl Sunday . . . the winter stonefly.

The winter stonefly isn't really one stonefly, but a collection of members from several families (Leuctridae, Capniidae, Nemouridae, and Taeniopterygidae) that look and behave superficially alike. Some people lump them into a group called the little dark stoneflies for obvious reasons. I'd like to call them poachers' stoneflies because they start emerging about the end of general trout season in November and end their hatch about the start of trout season in late April. It's a safe bet that the imitation is frequently cast over forbidden waters by sweaty-palmed lowlifes crouched behind granite boulders.

Winter stones are pretty weird. One member of the Capniidae family lives its entire life in the depths of Lake Tahoe. Even as an adult it never comes to the surface. Close relatives live in the splash zones of Lake Tahoe and other High Sierra lakes. Almost all other stoneflies require moving water.

People who study winter stoneflies are also pretty weird. Throughout the 1980s, Lisa and I would eagerly anticipate the annual January visit from our bug friends Dick Baumann and Riley Wilson. Dr. Baumann is one of the world's experts on stoneflies. His undergrad student Riley has since become an international authority on ants, but at the time his job was to drive Dick from Brigham Young University to the Tahoe Basin to study winter stoneflies.

In the foulest weather, the four of us would scramble and fall over Tahoe's ice-glazed boulders in search of the tiny black insects. Once we were thoroughly soaked, bruised, and frozen, we would wade through waist-deep snow and explore the lake's tributaries.

The only thing easy about the hunt was actually seeing the bugs. All winter stones are coal black. Immediately after hatching from nymphs that emerge along the water's edge, the adults start a furious march across the snow. They can fly and are attracted to lights, but like quail, they spend 99 percent of the time on their feet. When they stop moving, the sun warms their tiny black selves, and they melt into the snowpack. It is exactly this maneuver that allows the stoneflies to exist in an environment that would kill most other insects. Sierra air temperatures can drop below zero, but deep inside the insulating snow, the

Black winter stoneflies appear in stark contrast to their snowy domain. The cost of being conspicuously available to hungry birds apparently is outweighed by the advantage of thermal gain by the dark coloration. The thermal gain warms the stoneflies to the point that they melt into the snow, where they are insulated from the lethal cold of winter nights.

stoneflies bask in the relative warmth of a world that never drops much below freezing.

The average bug catcher would chase the obvious six-legged figures racing across the snow, but under the tutelage of our professor, we would simply tweeze the bugs out of their telltale pockmarks. We would hastily identify our captives and then drop them into alcohol-filled Nalgene phials for later enjoyment in a warm laboratory with hot drinks.

Despite the hundreds, even thousands, of winter stonefly nymphs that are readily found in the winter, they are often difficult to locate during summertime assays. The nymph has devised a survival strategy that is as wonderfully simple as it is effective. It buries deep within the streambed and estivates (goes dormant) during the summer. It can dig so deep into the water table that it is not uncommonly found in domestic well water. Not only does the nymph avoid the effects of water fluctuation, low oxygen, and heat, it also avoids having to compete with "summer" stones for available niches.

Winter stoneflies can hatch in bewildering numbers. At one location on Martis Creek, more than four hundred adults were found melted into a square meter of snow. Chickadees, gray-crowned rosy finches, and juncos often divulge the presence of a hatch as they feast on the bugs. With the tremendous concentration of nymphs, it is not surprising that trout move into the shallows and feed with gluttonous abandon during peak migration.

During these times, nymph imitations are the obvious choice, and a size 18 black Bird's Nest is really all you need. Not so obvious are the winter stone drys. On warm winter days, the snowbanks are continually sloughing into creeks, streams, and lakes. As often as not these clots of snow are riddled with adult winter stoneflies that can create minor feeding frenzies. A black Elk Hair or E/C Caddis is a dead ringer for the drubbed stones and will get bushwhacked in short order.

Another winter-hatching stonefly is the skwala. The skwala is much larger than the true winter stones, and its size 8 muddy brown imitation is large enough to bring frigid, otherwise lethargic trout to the surface. The skwala start hatching in January and will continue to emerge into April. These guys can emerge in

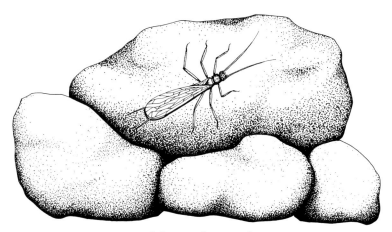

adult stonefly on rock

exceedingly large numbers. I remember waking on the East Carson and immediately pulling the sleeping bag back over my head after witnessing the silhouettes of hundreds of skwala clinging to my tent. The hatch increases in intensity as spring nears, and the best fishing is during those few weeks when the lowlands are warm but runoff hasn't yet begun. The adults are long-lived, and the prolonged hatching season makes this bug extremely important winter trout fare.

The Yuba River where it spills from the Western Sierra foothills is famous for its skwala hatches, but most winter stonefly opportunities are on the east slope of the Sierra, where the streams are open to winter fishing. The Truckee and Carson each support large populations of skwala, and their tributaries have zillions of the smaller winter stones. There are plenty of lakes in California that are legal to fish and have stonefly-friendly tributaries. If one of these is ice-free and near the town of Truckee, you may find my secret rock. If it is Superbowl Sunday, please stay home and enjoy the game.

39

Beneath the Mirror

This summer, I spent nearly two weeks, four to seven hours each day, observing from underwater an especially productive zone in an especially productive lake. At the end of the job, my mouth was frozen into the shape of a diving regulator, "U.S. Divers" was permanently stamped into my lip, and my skin had the look and texture of wrinkled Monterey Jack. There were creases around my eyes, my hair was falling out, and I had a beer belly—all likely caused by the long immersion.

In Hebgen Lake, at least, it was clear the fish and bugs hadn't read the textbooks, much less any of my articles. Their behavior at times defied logic, which I guess only means I was an idiot to ever imbue them with logic in the first place.

Earlier in this book was a chapter I wrote about *Callibaetis* mayflies. In the chapter, the nymphs obediently performed a daily dance at the bottom of the lake, and then against their better judgment got buoyed to the surface, where they hatched into duns, which flew away to live happily ever after for twenty-four

Nearly every western stillwater that supports trout also supports Callibaetis. *The clocklike hatch of* Callibaetis *conditions trout to actively seek emerging nymphs as they expose themselves above the weed beds in early to midmorning.*

hours. This is actually what happens much of the time, but I have observed so many exceptions to the rule that it is hard for me to believe that such a rule was conceived in the first place. But I'm as much to blame as anyone, because over the years, I have only casually watched the bugs rather than systematically observed them. For ease of understanding the *Callibaetis* game the way it is usually played, the *Callibaetis* chapter is left as is. Those of you fortunate enough to have read this far are going to learn the truth.

Almost half of the nymphs died en route to the surface. This wasn't at one time under one condition, but over the span of two weeks in conditions that ranged from hotter than hell and dead calm to wind-driven rain. Under all conditions, almost half of the nymphs never became duns. Contrary to what you might surmise, the fish didn't bother eating most of the nymphs; the dead bugs simply fell to the lakebed where, within a day or so, they became coated in a thick, white fungus.

The nymphs that invariably survived to become duns were *not* the nymphs that so characteristically "danced" above the weeds prior to upward migration. The nymphs that made it conserved their energy by carefully working their way to the tippy tops of the vegetation. Another strategy of those that made it was to launch from the bottom and aggressively swim to the surface. Again, those that resisted the upward pull of air entrained beneath their exoskeletons by swimming their way back down to the weeds when they got buoyed into open water ("dancing") were the ones that perished in the long run.

Most of the dancing is done at the start of the hatch. At this time, trout congregate along the bottom of the lake and inhale huge numbers of the bugs in exclusion of virtually any other food item present. As soon as the first nymphs start their aggressive swim from the bottom to the surface, perhaps 30 percent of the trout do likewise and resume their feeding at film level. Very soon after the aggressive swimmers start shooting to the surface, the dancing stops and the subsequent swimmer bugs begin a much slower ascent.

About 70 percent (these percentages are simply educated guesses) of the trout did *not* follow the fast-swimming nymphs to the surface but stayed low and converted to eating midge pupae. Once they converted to eating midges, they generally ignored the helpless, meaty, dying *Callibaetis* nymphs that were raining back down to the lakebed. Like I said, the actions of trout and bugs sometimes defy logic.

Like a powerful cataract that prevents the weaker steelhead from reaching their spawning beds, the lake's surface film separates the nymph nerds from the jocks. A nymph that can powerfully burst through the film in one or two tries has made a giant leap toward its ability to procreate. A wimpy nymph or one that has expended too much energy trying to hide in the weeds is doomed. "The meek shall inherit the earth" has a nice ring to it, but insects don't read the Bible any more than they read this book.

When the surface gets the slightest riffle on it, the nymphs brace against the film with their tails to help leverage themselves through the film. They create perfect U's, with their tail fibers spread to balance the load. This upward arching is *exactly opposite* from the "hunchback" emerger patterns that look so cool in the fly shop. The fish see this as well as I, and I would strongly hint that you save those hunchbacks for very calm waters.

When the wind starts to blow, the nymphs are in a world of hurt. The wind skates the top few millimeters of water over the calm water below. When a nymph tries to break through this shear, it gets tumbled relentlessly. Trout *love* these tumbling nymphs, and when it becomes Victory at Sea, instead of packing it in because the "rises have stopped," use an intermediate line and fish an unweighted Pheasant Tail Nymph on a 4X leader in the chop. Keep some slack in the system; the waves will make the presentation for you, and chop busters will reward with hard hits.

On hot days, emerging mayflies explode out of the nymphal shuck. I ascended alongside a *Callibaetis* nymph swimming to the surface. When it touched the film, instantly there was nothing but a hollow husk drifting under the surface. I was watching the whole thing through the viewfinder of my video camera and wrote it off as pointing the camera at the wrong bug when it approached the film. Back in the studio, I played the film, only to find that the camera had caught the action that was too swift for my bloodshot eyes to follow. In crisp detail, the video clearly shows the nymph's thorax cracking open and the mayfly being shoved out of the nymph apparently by internal gas pressure. A breeze caught the emerging wing, and the dun did a flip in the air and landed in the water on its back. After a few quick twitches, it hopped on its feet, shook its dazed little head, and flew away.

These same hot days relentlessly suck the energy out of spinners trying to lay their eggs. After one or two dips to the water, the spinner is toast and lies on the water waiting to die. On sweltering days, because of the difficult-to-catch emergers relative to the lazy abundance of spinners, trout frequently never become the slightest bit interested in emergers, but instead devote the entire rise period to spinners. On cool days, the opposite might be expected.

Spinner fishing on a lake is probably the ultimate challenge for the fly angler. In heavy spinner falls, trout have an unlimited opportunity to inspect the helpless creatures at their leisure. Dying spinners frequently vibrate their wings, and a subtle twitch on your line isn't a bad idea if you want to draw an uninterested fish in your direction. My good friend Phil Takatsuno has refined spinner fishing to an art form. He carries an array of patterns he is continually refining. His presentations are invariably flawless, and if he gets just a couple of refusals, he changes flies. Some trout are looking for a spinner with both wings in the air, some want one wing in the air, and of course, others will snub their noses at any spinner that isn't flat on the film.

Sometimes it is easier to simply watch than try to fish. You'll learn more that way, and no one can blame you for coming home empty-handed.

Index